ALSO BY EDUARDO GALEANO

# VOICES OF TIME

# VOICES OF TIME

## A LIFE IN STORIES

## OF

## TIME

### EDUARDO GALEANO

TRANSLATED BY MARK FRIED

METROPOLITAN BOOKS    HENRY HOLT AND COMPANY    NEW YORK

Metropolitan Books
Henry Holt and Company, LLC
*Publishers since 1866*
175 Fifth Avenue
New York, New York 10010

Metropolitan Books™ is a registered
trademark of Henry Holt and Company, LLC.

Originally published in Uruguay in 2004 under the title *Bocas del tiempo*
by Imprenta Rosgal S.A., Montevideo.

Library of Congress Cataloging-in-Publication Data
Galeano, Eduardo H., 1940–
    [Bocas del tiempo. English]
    Voices of time : a life in stories / by Eduardo Galeano ; translated by Mark
Fried.—1st American ed.
        p.  cm.
    ISBN-13: 978-0-8050-7767-4
    ISBN-10: 0-8050-7767-7
    1. Fried, Mark.  II. Title.
PQ8520.17.A4B6313    2006
863'.64—dc22                                                                    2005058048

Henry Holt books are available for special promotions and
premiums. For details contact: Director, Special Markets.

First American Edition 2006

Designed by Kelly S. Too

Printed in the United States of America

1  3  5  7  9  10  8  6  4  2

When they were still loose threads and not yet part of one cloth, a few of these stories were published in newspapers and magazines. In the process of weaving, the originals changed their color and shape.

This book recounts stories that I lived or heard.
In some of them, I name the sources. I would like also to thank the many sources who are not mentioned.

Images of the art of Peru's Cajamarca region accompany the text. These works, painted, etched, or carved anonymously, were collected by Alfredo Mires Ortiz in the course of many years of exploration and discovery. Some of them are thousands of years old but look as fresh as if they were made last week.

Inexplicably as always, Helena Villagra accompanied this book at every step. She partook of the stories told here, read and reread each of the pages, and helped both expunge the superfluous words and burnish those that were not.
Explicably as always, this book is dedicated to her.

EG
Montevideo, at the end of 2003

# CONTENTS

# VOICES OF TIME

# Time Tells

We are made of time.
We are its feet and its voice.
The feet of time walk in our shoes.
Sooner or later, we all know, the winds of time will erase the tracks.
Passage of nothing, steps of no one? The voices of time tell of the voyage.

# The Voyage

Oriol Vall, who works with newborns at a hospital in Barcelona, says that the first human gesture is the embrace. After coming into the world, at the beginning of their days, babies wave their arms as if seeking someone.

Other doctors, who work with people who have already lived their lives, say that the aged, at the end of their days, die trying to raise their arms.

And that's it, that's all, no matter how hard we strive or how many words we pile on. Everything comes down to this: between two flutterings, with no more explanation, the voyage occurs.

# Witnesses

The professor and the journalist walk in the garden.

The professor, Jean-Marie Pelt, stops, points, and says, "Allow me to introduce you to our grandparents."

The journalist, Jacques Girardon, crouches down and finds a ball of foam peeking out from the blades of grass.

The ball is a town of microscopic blue algae. On very humid days, the blue algae allow themselves to be seen. They look like a wad of spit. The French journalist wrinkles his nose; the origin of life isn't what we might call attractive, but from that spittle, from that mess, come all of us who have legs or roots or wings.

Before there was a before, when the world was barely a baby, without color or sound, there was blue algae. Streaming oxygen, they gave color to the sea and the sky. Then one fine day, a day that lasted millions of years, some blue algae decided to turn green. And bit by tiny bit, the green algae begat lichens, mushrooms, mold, medusas, and all the color and sound that came later, as did we, to unsettle the sea and the land.

Other blue algae preferred to carry on as they were.

And still are.

From the distant world that was, they observe the world that is.

What they think of it we do not know.

# Greeneries

When the sea became the sea, the land was still nothing but naked rock.

Then lichens, born of the sea, made meadows. They invaded the kingdom of stone, conquered it, turned it green.

That happened in the yesterday of yesterdays, and it is still going on. Lichens live where no one lives: on the frozen steppe, in the burning desert, on the peaks of the highest mountains.

Lichens live only as long as the marriage lasts between an alga and her son, the mushroom. If the marriage breaks up, the lichens break down.

Sometimes, fighting and disagreements lead the alga and mushroom to part. She complains that he keeps her hidden from the light. He says she makes him sick, feeding him sugar day and night.

# Footprints

A couple was walking across the savannah in East Africa at the beginning of the rainy season. The woman and the man still looked a lot like apes, truth be told, although they were standing upright and had no tails.

A nearby volcano, now called Sadiman, was belching ash. The rain of ash preserved the couple's footprints, from that moment through time. Beneath their gray blanket, the tracks remained intact. Those footprints show that this Eve and that Adam had been walking side by side; at a certain point she stopped, turned away, and took a few steps on her own. Then she returned to the path they shared.

The world's oldest human footprints left traces of doubt. A few years have gone by. The doubt remains.

# Time Plays Games

It's said that once upon a time two friends were admiring a painting. The work of art, by who knows who, was from China, a field of flowers at harvest time.

One of the friends, who knows why?, fixed his gaze on a figure in the painting, one of many women with baskets gathering poppies. She wore her hair loose, flowing over her shoulders.

At last she returned his gaze, let her basket fall, held out her arms, and, who knows how, carried him off.

He let himself be taken, who knows where, and with that woman he spent nights and days, who knows how many, until a gust of wind picked him up and returned him to the room where his friend remained standing before the painting.

So brief was that eternity that the friend had not noticed his absence. And neither had he noticed that the woman, one of many women in the painting gathering poppies in their baskets, now wore her hair tied at the back of her neck.

# Time Takes Its Time

He is one of the phantoms. That's what the people of Sainte Elie call the handful of old men, knee-deep in the mud, grinding stones and scraping sand in the abandoned mine that doesn't have a cemetery because even the dead don't want to stick around.

Half a century ago, a miner from far away arrived at the port of Cayena and set out to find the promised land. In those days, Sainte Elie was a garden ripening with golden fruit, where gold fattened many a starving stranger and sent him on his way back home, if the fates so wished it.

But the fates did not so wish it. The miner from far away is still here, wearing no more than a loincloth, eating nothing, eaten by mosquitoes. In search of nothing he stirs the sand day after day, seated beside his pan, under a tree even skinnier than he that barely offers any defense against the biting sun.

Sebastião Salgado reaches the lost mine, where no one visits, and sits at the miner's side. The gold digger has only one tooth, itself made of gold. When he speaks, the tooth shines in the night of his mouth. "My wife is very pretty," he says.

He digs out a blurry, dog-eared picture.

"She's waiting for me," he says.

She is twenty.

For half a century she's been twenty, somewhere in the world.

# Shipwrecked Words

After dark, Avel de Alencar worked away at his forbidden task.

Hiding in an office in Brasilia, night after night, he photocopied the military's secret archive: reports, dossiers, and files that called torture interrogation and murder confrontation.

In the three years of clandestine labor, Avel photocopied a million pages. The documents were a fairly complete confession by the military dictatorship then living out the final days of its absolute power over the lives and miracles of all Brazil.

One night, among the papers pulled from the files, Avel found a letter. The letter had been written ten years earlier, but the woman's kiss that signed off remained intact.

From then on, he came across many letters. Alongside each one was the envelope with the destination that they had never reached.

He did not know what to do. A lot of time had passed. No one was waiting for these letters now, words from the gone and forgotten sent to places and people no longer there. They were dead letters. And yet reading them felt to Avel like trespassing on something very much alive. He could not bring himself to return the words to the prison of the files, nor could he kill them by tearing up the pages.

At the end of each night, Avel put the letters in their envelopes, stuck on fresh stamps, and dropped them in the mailbox.

# Clinical History

She said she suffered from tachycardia every time she saw him, even from a distance.

She claimed that her salivary glands would go dry when he would look at her, even just a glance.

She admitted to a hypersecretion of the sweat glands each time he spoke to her, even just to return a greeting.

She acknowledged wild swings in her blood pressure when he would brush against her, even by mistake.

She confessed that because of him she suffered nausea, blurred vision, weak knees. During the day she could not stop from babbling stupidities and at night she could not sleep.

"That was a long time ago, doctor," she said. "I never felt it again."

The physician raised his eyebrows. "You never felt it ever again?"

He made his diagnosis: "Your case is serious."

# The Conjugal Institution

Captain Camilo Techera always went about with God on his lips: Good day, God willing. Until tomorrow, God willing.

When he took over the artillery base in Trinidad, he discovered that not a single soldier was married, as God commands, that all were living in sin, rolling in the hay of promiscuity like beasts in the field.

To put an end to this scandalous offense to the Lord, he sent for the priest who said mass in town. In a single day the priest ministered the holy sacrament of matrimony to all the troops, each with his girl, in the name of the captain, the Father, the Son, and the Holy Spirit.

From that Sunday on, all the soldiers were husbands.

On Monday, one soldier said, "That woman is mine."

And he buried a knife in the belly of a friend who had been looking at her.

On Tuesday, another soldier said, "This'll teach you."

And he wrung the neck of the woman who had vowed to obey him.

On Wednesday . . .

# Brawls and Squabbles

A derelict old man was selling contraband cigarettes from a little table in an alley in downtown Santiago, Chile. He was sitting on the ground, drinking from a bottle. I stopped to chat and accepted a sip of wine that promised instant cirrhosis.

As I was paying him for the cigarettes, a melee began. All at once the flies scattered, the wine capsized, the table collapsed, and a steamroller of a woman picked up the old man with one fist.

I bent to collect the cigarettes strewn on the ground, while the woman shook the bag of bones in her hand and screamed, You philandering cocksucker you Don Juan asshole who do you think you are you bare-faced swine so you've been screwing Eva and Lucy—and he muttered, I don't even know that one—and Pamela too—and he moaned, She came after *me*,—but the bombardment continued, You've been fucking Martha that bitch and that whore Charito and Betty and Patty, to the complete indifference of passersby, who showed no interest in this string of platinum blondes in fake eyelashes and reptilian boots.

While the indignant woman had her culprit by the throat and up against the wall, the man was mumbling vows, You are my only love you are my cathedral the others are nothing but little mission halls, until she, squeezing with intent to strangle, tossed him aside. Get out of here, she ordered. Get going, I never want to see you again. If I ever do . . ."

Without another word she pronounced her dreadful verdict. Her eyes fixed on his sacred parts, she scissored the air with her fingers.

Bravely, I edged away.

11

# The Seven Deadly Sins

Kneeling in the confessional, a repentant sinner admitted to greed, gluttony, lust, sloth, envy, pride, and anger.

"I've never confessed. I didn't want you priests enjoying my sins more than me, so out of greed I kept them to myself.

"Gluttony? From the moment I saw her, I confess, I wanted to eat her alive.

"Is it lust to enter someone and get lost inside and never find your way out?

"That woman was the only thing in the world that didn't make me slothful.

"I was envious—of myself, I confess.

"And I confess that later on I committed the sin of pride, believing she was me.

"And crazed with anger, I tried to break that mirror when I didn't see myself."

# Subsoil of the Night

Because the woman never shut up, because she was always complaining, because there was never a small misunderstanding that she didn't turn into a major problem, because he was tired of working like a mule for her and all her relatives, because he had to plead like a beggar in bed, because she had another and she pretended to be a saint, because she was a gnawing ache like nothing else he had ever felt, because he could not live without her or with her, he had no choice but to wring her neck like a chicken's.

Because the man never listened, because he never paid attention, because there was no major problem that he didn't treat like a small misunderstanding, because she was tired of working like a mule for him and all his relatives, because she had to obey like a whore in bed, because he had another and told the whole world, because he was a gnawing ache like nothing else she had ever felt, because she could not live without him or with him, she had no choice but to push him from the tenth floor like a sack of potatoes.

In the morning, they ate their breakfast. The radio was blaring the news like any other day. Nothing they heard caught their attention. Reporters don't cover dreams.

# Morals and Good Habits

They shut her up in a room, tied to the bed.
Every day a man entered, always the same one.
After a few months, the prisoner was pregnant.
Then they forced her to marry him.

The prison guards were not policemen or soldiers. They were the father and mother of the girl, practically a child, who had been caught kissing and stroking a classmate, another girl.

In Zimbabwe, at the end of 1994, Bev Clark heard her story.

# Fish

Mr. or Mrs.? Or both? Or sometimes a he and sometimes a she? In the depths of the sea, you can never tell.

Sea bass and other fish are virtuosos in the art of nonsurgical sex change. The girls become boys and the boys become girls with astonishing ease, with no condemnation or ridicule for betraying nature or God.

# Birds

The house, made of grass and twigs, is much larger than its inhabitant.

Building it in the thorny brush takes only a couple of weeks. Adorning it, however, demands much more time and effort.

No two houses are alike. Each home is painted to order, with pigment made of crushed berries, and each is decorated in its own way. The surroundings are dressed with treasures from the forest or from the detritus of some nearby town: pebbles, flowers, snail shells, weeds, mosses are laid out to create harmony, and beer-bottle caps and bits of colored glass, preferably blue, depict circles or fans on the ground. These designs are arranged and rearranged a thousand times until they occupy the best spots for catching the light.

Not for nothing are the birds called bowerbirds. They are the most flamboyant art architects in the islands of Oceania.

When the bird finishes building his home and garden, he lingers. He sings and waits for the females to pass by. For one of them to pause in its flight and admire his work. And then to choose him.

# Woodcocks

Winter gives way and the frozen mist melts in the beechwood forests of Asturias, where witches and owls build their nests.

That's when the woodcocks sing from their high perches. The cocks call to the hens and the hens respond. It's still dark when the song-soaked dance begins. Red faces, white beaks, black beards: the woodcocks and the woodhens sway like tiny carnival masks.

Hunters crouch in the forest, trigger fingers at the ready.

It's not easy to catch woodcocks, tucked away as they are in their hiding places, safe from all danger. But the hunters know that the birds become blind and deaf for the duration of this fiesta, the mating dance.

# Spiders

Step by tiny step, thread by tiny thread, the male spider approaches the female.

He offers her music, playing the web like a harp, and he dances for her while he caresses her bit by bit until her velvet body faints.

Then, before embracing her with all eight arms, the male wraps the female in his web and ties her up tight. Otherwise, she will devour him when the lovemaking is over.

The male spider loves and leaves before the prisoner awakens and insists on breakfast with the bed.

Who can fathom the fellow? He tied her to get astride her, escaped without dying inside her, and now he misses his darling spider.

# Serpents

Logs ablaze, sausages spitting juices; roast meat emitting the most sinful aromas. In front of his big stone house in the Sierra de Minas, deep in the forest, Don Venancio was throwing a barbecue for his friends from the city.

They were about to tuck in when the youngest son, still a boy, announced, "There's a snake in the house."

Raising a stick, he asked, "Shall I kill it?"

He was given the go-ahead.

A little later, Don Venancio went inside to check on the boy's work: it was a job well done. The head, now crushed by blows, still bore the mark of a yellow cross. It was a cross-snake, and a big one, measuring two yards, maybe three.

Don Venancio congratulated his son, served the meat, and sat down. The barbecue went on at length with seconds and thirds and much wine.

At the end, Don Venancio raised his glass to the matador, offering him the skin as a trophy, and he invited all to come and see. "It was enormous, the bitch."

But when they entered the house, the serpent was gone.

Don Venancio gnashed his teeth and said there was nothing to be done. "Her companion must have carried her off to their cave."

It's always that way, he said. Whether male or female, the widow or widower always comes for the dead.

Then everyone went back to the table, to the wine and the chatter and the jokes.

Everyone, except Pinio Ungerfeld, who told me this story. He could not. He remained in the house a long while, staring at the dry black stain on the floor.

# Afterlife

The sun is setting behind the cypresses when Aurora Meloni reaches the cemetery of San Antonio de Areco. They had phoned her. "We need the space. You understand, so many people dying."

An employee says, "Good afternoon, señora. That comes to three hundred pesos. Here you are."

And he hands her a plastic bag, the kind you use for putting out the garbage.

An enormous car is waiting.

The driver, dressed in black from cap to shoes, drives in silence. She appreciates the silence.

On the other side of the window the world flows by. In a field some boys play soccer. Aurora can't bear their insufferable joy, and she turns away. She watches the back of the driver's neck. She does not look at the bag, which is riding on the floor.

Who is inside the plastic bag? Is it Daniel? The boy who used to sell homemade cheese and custard with her in the streets of Montevideo? The one who swore he'd change the world and ended up in the gutter on a road like this one with thirty-six bullets in his body? Why didn't anyone warn them that it would all be over so quickly? Where are the words they never got to say? What about the things they never got to do?

The gunmen, the murderers in uniform, are still there, right where they were. But where is she? In this never-ending car ride, this rented funereal float? Is she here? Is she this woman who bites her lip and feels her eyes stinging? Is this a car? Or is it a phantom train that one day jumped the tracks and carried her off to nowhere?

# Time Plays Tricks

Squatting on the bed, she gazed at him, her eyes sliding over his nakedness, from head to toe, slowly, as if scrutinizing each freckle, and she said, "The only thing I'd change is your address."

From then on they lived together and enjoyed fighting over the paper at breakfast and cooking crazy concoctions and sleeping wrapped around each other.

Suddenly half of all that was gone.

Now this mutilated man, this he without she, tries to recall her as she was. As any of the many women she was, each with her own grace and power, because she had the astonishing habit of being reborn.

But no. Memory refuses. He can't remember anything but an icy body empty of all the women she was.

# Unibody

With the help of their white canes and a few drinks, they groped their way through the narrow streets of Tlaquepaque.

It seemed they were about to fall, but no. Whenever she stumbled, he righted her; whenever he swayed, she steadied him. They walked as a duo, and as a duo they sang. They always stopped at the same spot in the shade of the portico, and with strained voices they sang old Mexican tunes about love and war. They used some instrument, maybe a guitar, I can't recall, to compound the racket. And between songs they'd rattle the bowl in which they collected coins from their faithful public.

Then they'd head off. Preceded by their canes, they would push through the crowd and be lost in the distance, a ragged, battered pair, each huddled tightly against the other, together as one in their shared patch of darkness under the sun.

# The Kiss

Antonio Pujía randomly picked out one of the blocks of Carrara marble he'd been buying over the years.

It was a tombstone, from a grave that lay who knows where. He hadn't the slightest idea how it had ended up in his workshop.

Antonio laid the tombstone down on a support base and set to work. He had a vague idea of what he wanted to carve, or maybe he had none. He began by erasing the inscription: the name of a man, the year of his birth, the year of his death.

Then the chisel entered the stone. Inside Antonio found a surprise waiting for him: the vein of the marble took the shape of two profiles meeting, eye to eye, something like two faces joined at the forehead, nose, and mouth.

The sculptor obeyed, carefully excavating until the encounter within the stone emerged.

The next day he figured his work was done. And then, when he lifted the tombstone, he saw what he hadn't seen before. On the back of the stone was another inscription: the name of a woman, the year of her birth, the year of her death.

# The Oldest Man in the World

It was summer, and Don Francisco Barriosnuevo had been there for countless summers past.

"He's a glutton for years," said the woman next door. "Older than a tortoise."

The neighbor was scaling a fish with a knife, flies were rubbing their legs in anticipation of the feast, and Don Francisco was drinking guava juice. Gustavo Tatis, who had come from far away, shouted questions into his ear.

The world was still, the air was still. In the town of Majagual, a hamlet lost in the swamps, everyone else was taking a siesta.

Gustavo asked Don Francisco about his first love. He had to repeat the question several times, first love, *first love*, FIRST LOVE. Methuselah cupped his ear with his hand. "What? What did you say?"

And at last, "Oh, yes."

Rocking in his chair, he wrinkled his brow, closed his eyes. "My first love . . ."

Gustavo waited. He waited while memory traveled. And that creaky little boat listed, shipped water, got lost. It took a voyage of more than a century, and the waters were shrouded in mist. Don Francisco went in search of his first time, his faced screwed up, pitted by a thousand furrows. Gustavo looked away and waited.

At last Don Francisco murmured, almost secretly, "Isabel."

Then he rammed his bamboo cane into the ground, and leaning on it he rose up from his chair, arched his back like a rooster, and howled, "Isabe-e-e-l!"

# Time Turns Pages

"When?" she asked. "When?"

Once a week, Miguel Migliónico passed by her doorway. He always found her sitting there, facing the street, and Doña Elvirita always peppered him with questions about his wife's pregnancy. "When?"

And Miguel repeated, "June."

White attire always neat, white hair always combed, Doña Elvirita radiated peace, the dignity of age, and she dispensed advice: "Touch her belly, it brings good luck."

"Tell her to drink dark beer or malteds, so she'll have lots of milk."

"Give her what she hankers for, each and every craving, because if a woman has to swallow her hunger the kid gets birthmarks."

Every Friday, Doña Elvirita awaited Miguel's appearance. Her translucent skin, which encircled her body like pink smoke, revealed a tangle of little veins popping with curiosity. "And her belly, is it pointed? Then for sure it's a boy."

Winds from the south blew cold, autumn was leaving the streets of Montevideo.

"It won't be long now, right?"

One afternoon, Miguel came by in a great hurry. "The doctor says it's a matter of hours. Today or tomorrow."

Doña Elvirita opened her eyes wide. "Already?"

The following Friday her chair was empty. Doña Elvirita died on June 17, 1980, while in the Migliónico home a boy named Martín was born.

# Mother

A sneaker,
a love letter, signature illegible,
ten little pots with plastic flowers,
seven balloons in assorted colors,
an eyeliner pencil,
a glove,
a cap,
an old photo of Alan Ladd,
three Ninja turtles,
a storybook,
a maraca,
fourteen hairbrushes,
and a few toy cars
are part of the booty of a cat that lives and steals in the Avel-
laneda neighborhood.

Slinking along rooftops and cornices, she steals for her son, who
is paralyzed and lives surrounded by these ill-gotten offerings.

# Father

Vera stayed home from school and spent the entire day indoors. At dusk, she wrote her father a letter. He was in the hospital, quite ill. She wrote, "You must like yourself, take care of yourself, look out for yourself, spoil yourself, forgive yourself, love yourself, cherish yourself. I'll like you, I'll take care of you, I'll look out for you, I'll spoil you, I'll forgive you, I'll love you, I'll cherish you."

Héctor Carnevale lasted a few days more. Then, with his daughter's letter under his pillow, he departed in his sleep.

# Grandmother

When Miriam Míguez looks at a mountain, she wishes she could pass through it with her gaze and come out on the other side of the world. When she looks at her childhood, she wishes she could pass through all the years and come out on the other side of time.

On the other side of time is Grandmother.

In her house in Córdoba, Grandmother kept a few boxes hidden away. Sometimes, when Miriam and she were alone and there was no danger that anyone might walk in, Grandmother would crack open her treasure chests and let her grandchild see inside.

Those sequins, tiny medals, bird feathers, old keys, knitting needles, colored ribbons, dry leaves, and magazine clippings looked like mere things, but the two of them knew they were much more than things.

When Grandmother died, it all disappeared, perhaps burned or put out with the trash.

Now Miriam has secret boxes of her own. Sometimes she opens them.

# Grandfather

Geologists were searching for the remains of a small copper mine called Cortadera, which had once existed but no longer appeared on any map.

In the town of Cerrillos someone told them, "No one knows anything about that. Who could say? Maybe old Honorio knows."

Don Honorio, defeated by aches and pains and wine, greeted the geologists from his cot. They had a hard time convincing him. Only after a goodly number of bottles and many cigarettes—I think so, I don't know, we'll see—did the old man agree to accompany them the following day.

Dog-tired, stumbling, he began to walk.

At first he languished at the back. He refused any assistance, and they had to wait for him to catch up. With a great effort he managed to reach the dry riverbed.

Then, bit by bit, his gait grew steadier. Along the length of the gully and across the stony fields his bent body began to straighten.

"Over there! Over there!" He pointed the way, and his voice came alive when he recognized long-lost places.

After a full day's hike, Don Honorio, who had started in silence, was doing most of the talking. He climbed hills and leaped over years. By the time they entered the valley, he was marching ahead of his young, exhausted companions.

He slept with his face to the stars. He was the first one up, anxious to get to the mine, and he brooked no detour or distraction.

"That's the grinder and there's the steam shovel," he said. And without the least hesitation, he located the mouths of shafts and the places that once boasted the best veins, the rusty irons that used to be machinery, the ruins that were homes, the parched corners once fed by springs. For each spot, each object, Don Honorio had a story, and every story overflowed with people and laughter.

By the time they arrived back in town, he was younger than his grandchildren.

# Labor

At dawn Doña Tota walked into a hospital in the barrio of Lanús. She was carrying a child in her belly. In the entranceway she found a star, in the form of a brooch, lying on the floor.

The star sparkled on one side, but not the other. That happens whenever stars fall to earth and lay in the dirt. On one side they glow silver, invoking the nights of the world; on the other side, they're just tin.

Gripped in her fist, that star of silver and tin accompanied Doña Tota in labor.

The newborn was named Diego Armando Maradona.

# Birth

The public hospital in the fanciest neighborhood of Rio de Janeiro received a thousand patients every day. Nearly all were poor or poorer.

A doctor on call told Juan Bedoian, "Last week, I had to choose between two newborns. We have only one incubator. The babies came at the same time, each with one foot in the grave, and I had to choose which would live and which would die."

This isn't up to me, the doctor thought. Let God decide.

But God paid no heed.

Whatever he did, he was going to commit a crime. If he did nothing, he'd commit two.

No time to dither. The newborns were slipping away.

The doctor closed his eyes. One baby was condemned to die; the other was condemned to live.

# Baptism

A ferocious storm was pelting Buenos Aires.

The father yanked the baby from his mother's arms, carried him to the roof, and raised him high and naked in the freezing rain. Amid flashes of lightning, he cried out, "My son, may the waters of heaven bless you!"

No one knows just how, but the newborn managed to keep from dying of pneumonia.

He also escaped the name Sunday Rest. His father, a poor anarchist and poet eternally pursued by creditors and the police, had chosen the name in homage to the workers' latest victory, but the civil registry refused. So he got together with his friends, also poor anarchists and poets eternally pursued by creditors and the police, to discuss the matter. They decided the boy would lead a literary life and that he deserved the name Catulo, after the Roman poet Catullus.

At the civil registry, they added an accent to Cátulo Castillo, who went on to write "La última curda" and other tangos of the sort people listen to standing up, hat in hand.

# Christening

The town of Stubby Hill never had a hill, stubby or otherwise. But Javier Zeballos remembers from his childhood that it had three constables, three judges, and three doctors.

One of the doctors, who lived downtown, was the needle on the compass. Javier's mother would give her son directions: "From Dr. Galarza's house, go down two blocks." Or, "That's up the street from Dr. Galarza's." Or, "Go to the drugstore around the corner from Dr. Galarza."

And off Javier would march. Whenever he went, under sun or moon, Dr. Galarza was always seated on the porch, yerba maté gourd in hand, responding politely to his neighbors' greetings: "Good morning, Doctor." "Good afternoon, Doctor." "Good evening, Doctor."

Javier was a grown man when it occurred to him to ask why Dr. Galarza had no office or clinic. That's when he found out. The man was no doctor; he was Doctor. Given name, Doctor; family name, Galarza.

His father yearned for a son with a diploma and didn't think the baby could be trusted.

# Birthday

Face of a happy ant, butt of a frog, legs of a chicken: Sally had her first birthday.

The event was celebrated in a big way. Her mother, Beatriz Monegal, spread over the floor an enormous embroidered floral tablecloth, whose origin could not be divulged, and lit the small candle on the cake from the Sandwich Emporium for which she would never pay.

In one amen the cake was gone and the dancing began. Meanwhile, the birthday girl slept deeply, wrapped in clean starched clothes in a shopping basket.

At a quarter to three in the morning, not a drop left in the jugs of wine, Beatriz snapped her last photographs, switched off the radio, shooed everyone out, and hurriedly picked up all her things.

At three on the dot came the wail of a police siren. Beatriz had moved into that big house a couple of months before, along with her many children and her most recent love, a muscular man good at kicking down doors. When the police arrived to serve the eviction notice, Beatriz was already off on a new pilgrimage.

She paraded down the middle of the street, hauling a cart crammed with little children and rags, followed by her man and her older children. She was on the lookout for another house, and laughing a laugh that cracked the silence of the Montevideo night.

# Revelation

A recent arrival in the world was sleeping naked in his crib.

His sister, Ivonne Galeano, took one look and ran out. She knocked on her girlfriends' doors and finger to lips invited them to the show. They abandoned their dolls half dressed, half combed, and holding hands, standing on tiptoe, they peeked inside the crib. None of them flushed with envy or blanched with fear. Stifling giggles, they cried, "Look what this nutcase brought along to pee with!"

# Wind

The morning Diego López turned four, joy was leaping in his breast, a flea jumping on a frog hopping on a kangaroo bouncing on a pogo stick, while the streets flew on the wind and wind battered the windows. Diego hugged his grandma Gloria and whispered a secret order in her ear: "We're going into the wind."

And he pulled her from the house.

# Sun

Somewhere in Pennsylvania, Anne Merak works as an assistant to the sun.

She's been in that line of work for as long as she can recall. At the end of every night, Anne raises her arms and pushes the sun up into the sky. Lowering her arms at day's end she puts the sun down to bed on the horizon.

She was very small when she started this job, and she's never missed a shift.

Half a century ago, she was declared insane. Since then Anne has gone through several institutions, been treated by numerous psychiatrists, and swallowed innumerable pills.

They never managed to cure her.

Thank heavens.

# Eclipse

When the moon blocks the sun, the Kayapó people shoot flaming arrows into the sky to return to the sun its lost light. The Barí people play drums to make the sun reappear. The Aymaras cry, scream, and beg the sun not to abandon them.

At the end of '94, there was panic in Potosí. Night fell in the middle of the morning, the sky suddenly black and starry. In that dead-cold, end-of-time world, Indians cried, dogs howled, birds hid, and in one amen the flowers wilted.

Helena Villagra was there. When the eclipse ended, she felt something missing from her ear. An earring, a little silver sun. She searched for it on the ground for a long time, even though she knew she would never find that little sun.

# Night

Back when she was a child, Helena pretended to be sleeping and then slipped out of bed.

She dressed all in white, as if it were Sunday, and without a sound snuck out to the patio to discover the mysteries of the Tucumán night.

Her parents slept, her sisters as well.

She wanted to see how the night changed and how the moon and stars moved. Someone had told her that the heavenly bodies shifted and sometimes fell, and that as the night advanced they changed color.

That night of nights, Helena watched without blinking. Her neck ached, her eyes hurt. She rubbed her eyes and looked again. She looked and kept on looking, but the sky did not change and the moon and the stars remained firmly in their places.

Dawn awakened her. Helena shed a tear.

Later, she consoled herself with the thought that night doesn't like anyone spying on its secrets.

# Moon

The gibbous moon impregnates the earth, so the felled tree may live on in its wood.

The full moon sends lunatics, dreamers, women, and the sea into a frenzy.

The green moon kills the crops.

The yellow moon comes laden with storm.

The red moon brings war and plague.

The black moon, no moon at all, leaves the world sad and the sky mute.

Taking her first steps, Catalina Álvarez Insúa raised her arms to the moonless sky and called, "Moon, come!"

# Light Dwellers

Catalina had many visible friends, but they weren't portable.

The invisible ones, on the other hand, went with her everywhere. She said there were twenty. She couldn't count any higher.

No matter where, she took them along. She'd pull them out of her pocket, put them in the palm of her hand, and talk to them.

Then she'd say bye, see you tomorrow, and she'd blow them toward the sun.

The invisible ones slept in the light.

# Morgan

The sun corners him; Morgan gets away. He flies over the sand, swerves around the waves, and you feel like applauding.

But Morgan's name comes from his pirate ways, and his victims are less admiring. Pouncing and stealing, Morgan gets chased not only by the sun but by the owner of the tennis ball or sandwich or sneaker or underwear he grabs before diving under water, booty between his teeth.

He's never managed to mend his manners. No one has ever seen him sit still or show even the slightest hint of fatigue or regret.

Morgan had been making his dogged way in the world for four years when Manuel Monteverde, the same age, sat on a rock and thought about it. "Yes," he decided. "Morgan misbehaves. But he makes you laugh."

# Leo

For Ricardo Marchini the moment of truth had arrived.

"Come on, Leo," he said. "We have to talk."

And off they went up the street, the two of them. They wandered for a while around Saavedra, turning corners in silence. As usual, Leonardo fell behind, then had to hurry to catch up to Ricardo, who walked with his hands in his pockets and his brow furrowed.

At the plaza, Ricardo sat down. He swallowed. He took Leonardo's face in his hands, looked into his eyes, and let loose a torrent: "Look Leo forgive me for telling you but you're not Mom's and Dad's and Leo better you should know the facts you got picked up off the street."

He took a deep breath. "I had to tell you, Leo."

Leonardo had been plucked out of a garbage can as a newborn, but Ricardo spared him that detail.

Then they went back home.

Ricardo was whistling.

Leonardo stopped at the foot of his favorite trees, greeted the neighbors by wagging his tail, and barked at the fleeing shadow of a cat.

The neighborhood loved him because he was brown and white, same as the Platense, the local soccer team that almost never won.

# Lord Chichester

In one of the many parking lots of Buenos Aires, Raquel heard him cry. Someone had tossed him between two cars.

He joined the household, was named Lord Chichester. He'd been born not long ago, and his fur was dull and his head was big. He ended up one-eyed later on, after he grew up and fought a duel over the she-cat Milonga.

One night, wild screeching tore Raquel and Juan Amaral from the deepest of slumbers. It sounded like Lord Chichester was being skinned alive. Strange, since though ugly he was usually quiet.

"Something hurts bad," said Juan.

They followed the yowls to the end of the corridor. Raquel listened closely. "He's letting us know there's a leak."

They wandered about the big old house until they found the gloop-gloop of a drip in the bathroom. "That pipe always dripped," said Juan.

"It's going to flood," Raquel feared.

And they discussed it—yes, no, who knows?—until Juan looked at his watch, nearly five in the morning, and yawning he begged, "Let's go back to sleep."

And he concluded, "Lord Chichester is nuts."

They were about to enter the bedroom, still persecuted by the cat's screeching, when the old, cracked ceiling above their bed collapsed.

# Pepa

Pepa Lumpen was worn down by the years. She no longer barked, and when she tried to walk, she fell over. Martinho the cat came up close and licked her face. Pepa had always put him in his place, growling and showing her teeth, but that last day she let herself be kissed.

The house went quiet, emptied of her.

In the nights that followed, Helena dreamed she was cooking in a pot with a broken bottom, and that Pepa called her on the phone, furious because we'd put her underground.

# Pérez

When Mariana Mactas turned six, a neighbor on Calella de la Costa gave her a little blue chick. Not only did the chick have blue feathers, which gave off violet sparks in the sunlight, it also peed blue pee and peeped blue peeps. A miracle of nature, helped along perhaps by an injection of blue dye in the egg.

Mariana baptized it Pérez. They were friends. They spent hours chatting on the terrace while Pérez walked about pecking at bread-crumbs.

The chick didn't last long. And when that brief blue life came to an end, Mariana lay sprawled on the floor as if she would never get up again. Staring at a tile, she intoned, "Poor world without Pérez."

# Curious People

Soledad, five, daughter of Juanita Fernández: "Why don't dogs eat dessert?"

Vera, six, daughter of Elsa Villagra: "Where does night sleep? Does night sleep here under the bed?"

Luis, seven, son of Francisca Bermúdez: "Will God be angry if I don't believe in him? I don't know how to tell him."

Marcos, nine, son of Silvia Awad: "If God made himself, how did he make his back?"

Carlitos, forty, son of María Scaglione: "Mama, how old was I when you weaned me? My psychiatrist wants to know."

# The Rate of Infant Immortality

When Manuel was a year and a half, he wanted to know why he couldn't hold water in his hand. And when he was five, he wanted to know why people die: "What is dying?"

"My grandma died because she was old? So why did a kid younger than me die? I saw it yesterday on TV."

"Sick people die? So why do people who aren't sick die?"

"Do dead people die for a while, or do they die for good?"

At least Manuel had an answer for the question that most troubled him: "My brother Felipe is never going to die because he always wants to play."

# Whispers

Luiza Jaguaribe was playing in the yard of her house on the outskirts of Passo Fundo. Jumping on one foot, she counted the buttons on her dress: "One, two. The captain will do."

Counting buttons, she tried to guess which husband fate would bring her. Would she marry the captain or the king, with a bonnet or a ring? "Three, four. A bonnet I'll adore."

"Five, six. The captain plays tricks."

She leaped spinning into the air, spread her arms, and sang, "The king will give a ball. 'Cause I counted them all!"

When she spun around, she bumped into her father's legs and fell to the ground. Her father, immense against the sun, said, "Enough, Luizinha. It's over."

That's how she learned Uncle Moro was no more.

He went to Heaven, they told her. And they told her she had to stay still and not speak.

A few days went by, the holidays came.

That Christmas Eve the entire family got together. Luiza met relatives she'd never seen before, a crowd dressed in mourning.

Aunt Gisela sat at the head of an endless table. She looked beautiful in her black dress with the high buttoned collar, a queen. But Luiza didn't dare tell her so.

Her head held high, her gaze fixed on nothing, Aunt Gisela did not eat a thing or say a word. Then at midnight, right in the midst of all the hubbub, she spoke: "They say we have to love God. I hate him."

She said it softly, almost mouthing the words. Only Luiza heard her.

# Bad Words

Ximena Dahm was very nervous, for that morning she was to begin her life at school. She dashed from one mirror to another, and in one of her comings and goings she tripped over a bag and fell down. She didn't cry, but she was mad: "What's this piece of crap doing here?"

Her mother chided her: "Honey, you know we don't say that word."

Ximena, from the floor, wanted to know, "What are good words that we don't say?"

# Useful Lessons

Joaquín de Souza is learning to read, and he practices with the signs he sees. He thinks the most important word in the world is no, because everything begins with it.

"No trespassing."

"No dogs allowed."

"No littering."

"No smoking."

"No spitting."

"No parking."

"No loitering."

"No campfires."

"No noise."

"No . . ."

# Rules

Chema was playing with a ball, the ball was playing with Chema. The ball was a world of colors, and the world was flying free and wild, floating on air, bouncing wherever it wished. It touched down here, leaped over there, bounced and bounced until it reached his mother and came to a halt.

Maya López took the ball and locked it away. She said Chema was a menace to the furniture, to the house, to the neighborhood, and to all of Mexico City, and she made him put on his shoes, sit down properly, and do his homework.

"Rules are rules," she said.

Chema raised his head: "I have my rules too." And in his opinion a good mother should obey her son's rules.

"Let me play all I want, let me go barefoot, don't ever make me go to school, don't make me go to bed early, and we'll move to a new house every day."

Then, eyes on the ceiling and in a tone of feigned indifference, he added, "And be my girlfriend."

# Good Health

At the busstop a swarm of youngsters crowded on board. Loaded down with books and notebooks and other stuff, they filled the bus with nonstop chatter and laughter. Talking all at once, shouting, pushing, showing off, they laughed at anything and everything.

A man scolded Andrés Bralich, one of the loudest: "What's wrong with you, kid? You got laughing sickness?"

Just one glance was enough to confirm that all the other passengers had been treated in time and were in full remission.

# The Teacher

The sixth graders at a school in Montevideo held a novel-writing competition.

Everyone took part.

Three of us were on the jury: Oscar, teacher of the threadbare cuffs and a fakir's wages, a student representing the authors, and me.

At the awards ceremony, no parents or other adults were allowed in. We the members of the jury read out our decision, which praised the merits of each and every submission. Everyone won, and for every winner there was an ovation, a downpour of streamers, and a little medal donated by a local jeweler.

Afterward Oscar told me, "We feel so connected to each other. I'd like to keep them all back."

One of the girls, who had moved here from a small town in the country, stayed to chat. She told me she never used to open her mouth, and with a laugh she said now the problem was she couldn't shut up. She loved her teacher, she said, loved him very very very much, because he'd taught her not to be afraid of being wrong.

# The Students

When the teacher asks the girls what they want to be when they grow up, they don't answer. Then, quietly, they confess: I want to be whiter, sing on TV, sleep in till noon, marry a guy who won't beat me, marry a guy with a car, go far away where nobody will ever find me.

The boys say: I want to be whiter, be a soccer star, be Spiderman and walk up walls, rob a bank and never have to work, buy a restaurant and get to eat all the time, go far away where nobody will ever find me.

They live quite close to the city of Tucumán, but they've never seen it. Arriving by foot or on horseback, they attend school one day then skip the next two, taking turns with their siblings to wear the only pair of shoes. And the question they most often ask the teacher is, When is lunch coming?

# Condors

By mule, motorcycle, or on his own two feet, Federico Ocaranza roams the mountains of Salta. He heals mouths in those desolate, destitute places. A visit from the dentist, pain's nemesis, is good news, and up there good news is as scarce as everything else.

Federico plays soccer with the children, who rarely see the inside of a school. They learned what they know by herding goats and chasing a rag ball in their world amid the clouds.

Between goals they have fun teasing the condors. Lying flat on the rocky ground, arms spread-eagled, they pretend to be dead. Then, when the condors attack, the little corpses jump up and run away.

# Manpower

Mohammed Ashraf doesn't go to school.

From sun-up till moonrise, he measures, cuts, shapes, punctures, and sews soccer balls, which then go rolling out from the Pakistani village of Umar Kot toward the stadiums of the world.

Mohammed is eleven. He has been at this since he was five.

If he knew how to read, and could read English, he would understand the label he sticks on each of his products: "This ball was not made by children."

# Recompense

Homeless and aimless, with neither a where nor a why, José Antonio Gutiérrez grew up on the streets of Guatemala City.

To dodge hunger, he stole. To dodge loneliness, he sniffed glue and imagined himself a Hollywood star.

One day he took off north, headed for Paradise. Dodging the police, sneaking on train after train, and hiking a thousand and one nights, he found his way to California. And there he stayed.

Six years later, in Guatemala's most wretched barrio, a loud knocking woke Engracia Gutiérrez. Several men in uniform stood at the door. They'd come to tell her that her brother, José Antonio of the U.S. Marines, had died in Iraq.

The kid from the streets was the first casualty of the invading forces in the year 2003.

The authorities wrapped his coffin in the Stars and Stripes and gave him military honors. And they made him a U.S. citizen, which was the reward they'd promised.

During the live funeral broadcast, they praised the heroism of the valiant soldier fallen in combat against Iraqi troops.

Later it came out that he was killed by "friendly fire," which is what they call the bullets that get the wrong enemy.

# The Horse

Every afternoon, Paulo Freire snuck into the movie theater in Recife's Casa Forte neighborhood to see Tom Mix. He watched, eyes wide and unblinking, day after day.

The feats of the cowboy in the broad-brimmed hat who rescued damsels in distress were entertaining enough, but what Paulo really liked was the way his horse sailed along. From so much time spent peering at the horse and revering him, the two became friends, and Tom Mix's horse stayed with Paulo for the rest of his life.

Paulo traveled a great deal. His work as a revolutionary educator, a man who taught by learning, took him around the world. Down all the roads and throughout all the years of awards and adversity, that horse the color of light galloped tirelessly on in his memory and in his dreams.

Paulo searched everywhere for those movies from his childhood. "Tom who?" No one had a clue.

Then at last, at the age of seventy-four, he found them somewhere in New York. And he watched them once again. It was unbelievable: his faithful friend the shimmering horse was nothing at all like Tom Mix's, not even close.

Faced with this painful revelation, Paulo murmured, "It doesn't matter . . . But it does."

# The Final Prank

The children of Brazil learned to be Brazilians and magicians from hearing or reading the stories of Monteiro Lobato. When he died, they all became orphans.

But the children of Brazil did not attend the funeral. Two adults offered eulogies, and each claimed Monteiro Lobato for his own political party: Rossini Camargo Guarnieri bid farewell to his Communist comrade, and Phebus Gicovate paid homage to his fellow Trotskyite.

As soon as the funeral speeches ended, the two squared off. They argued in the plural, as befits questions of world revolution:

"Renegades!"

"Divisionists!"

"Bureaucrats!"

"Provocateurs!"

"Usurpers!"

"Traitors!"

"Murderers!"

Back and forth the charges flew, the heat of ideological debate rising until the men came to blows. Punching wildly, the two tumbled right into the open grave.

Dona Purezinha, the widow, threw up her arms and implored them to show some respect for the dead. She didn't realize that Monteiro Lobato was dying all over again, this time from laughter. He was the one directing the brawl.

# A Bottle Adrift

That morning, Jorge Pérez lost his job. He was given no explanation, nothing to soften the blow. Without warning, after years at the oil refinery, he was simply given the boot.

He walked away, not knowing why or where to, obeying legs more alive than he was. At a time of day when nothing in the world casts a shadow, his legs carried him along the southern shore of Puerto Rosales.

At a bend in the river, he spied a bottle in among the bulrushes. Corked and sealed shut, it seemed a gift from God to take the edge off his gloom. But once he'd wiped off the mud, Jorge saw the bottle contained paper, not wine.

He let it drop and went on.

Then he retraced his steps.

He broke the neck of the bottle on a rock and pulled out several water-stained drawings. They were sketches of suns and seagulls, flying suns, glowing gulls. There was a letter too, come from afar on the sea, and it was addressed to The Finder of This Message:

Hi, I'm Martín.
I'm ate years old.
I like kookies, fride eggs and the color green.
I like to draw.
I want a friend on the waterway.

# On the Waterfront

He seemed like a really nice kid. Though they'd only just met, the boy who sold crabs on the beach invited Caetano for a ride in his boat.

"I'd like to," Caetano said, "but I can't. I've got a lot to do. Errands . . ."

But they went. By boat they went to the market and the bank, the post office, and other places. All along the waterfront they entered the city from the shore, and to prolong the simple pleasure of looking at it, they took their time floating on the calm sea.

Thus was San Salvador de Bahía discovered anew. Suffering the relentless racket of the city by foot was one thing. The city by boat was truly something else. Caetano Veloso had never seen it like that, from the wet, from the quiet.

At the end of the afternoon the boat dropped Caetano off back at the beach where he'd embarked. He wanted to know the name of the boy who'd revealed this other city that the city was. Standing in his boat, his black body gleaming in the sun's last rays, the boy said: "My name is Marco Polo. Marco Polo Mendes Pereira."

# Water

At the beginning of time, the ant's waist was not narrow.

It's all in Genesis, in the version that circulates by word of mouth on Colombia's Pacific coast. The ant was round and filled with water.

But God had forgotten to water the world. Realizing his blunder, he asked for help. The ant refused.

Then God's fingers pinched his belly.

Thus were born all the rivers and the seven seas.

# Water Lords

There are companies just like the ant, only they're much larger.

At the end of the twentieth century a water war broke out in the city of Cochabamba.

The U.S. company Bechtel took over the water system and tripled the rates overnight. Indigenous communities marched in from the valleys and blockaded the city, which also rebelled, raising barricades and burning water bills in a great bonfire in the Plaza de Armas.

The Bolivian government answered with bullets, as usual. There was a state of siege, people were killed and imprisoned, but the uprising continued day after day, night after night, for two months unstoppable, until with a final push the people of Cochabamba won back the liquid that nourishes their bodies and sustains their crops.

In the city of La Paz, however, protests failed to stop the French company Suez from taking over the water system. Rates skyrocketed, and practically no one could afford to turn on the tap. Why was consumption so low? European experts and government officials wondered. Cultural backwardness, obviously. Poor people, which means just about everybody in Bolivia, don't know enough to bathe every day the way people have in Europe for maybe the last quarter of an hour, and they don't realize they need to wash the cars they don't have.

# Brands

With a wave of the hand the customer declined the glass of tap water and summoned the sommelier, who read out a long list of bottled waters.

The table tried a few brands not well known in California, at about seven dollars a bottle.

While they ate, they went through several bottles. Amazonas from the Brazilian jungle was very good, and the Spanish water from the Pyrenees was excellent, but best of all was the French brand Eau de Robinet.

The *robinet* is where they all came from: the faucet. The bottles, with labels made up by a friendly printer, had been filled in the kitchen.

The meal was filmed by a hidden camera in a chic Los Angeles restaurant. And Penn and Teller showed it on TV.

# The Fountain

In the twelfth century, when water was free like the air and un-labeled, the pope and a fly met up at a fountain.

Pope Adrian IV, the only English pontiff in the history of the Vatican, lived a hectic life due to incessant wars against William the Bad and Frederick Red Beard. Of the fly's life, nothing is known worth mentioning.

By divine intervention or destiny's design, their paths crossed at the fountain in the plaza of the town of Agnani, one summer noon in the year 1159.

The Holy Father, who was thirsty, opened his mouth to drink and the fly went down his throat. It was a mistake, for there was nothing of interest down there, but once inside neither the fly's wings nor the pope's fingers could get him out.

In the struggle, both of them met their fate. The choking pope died of a fly. The imprisoned fly died of a pope.

# The Lake

Holden Caulfield's history teacher was berating him for his shortcomings. To escape this distressing catalog, Holden thought about the ducks in New York's Central Park. Where did they go in the winter when the lake iced over? A much more interesting topic than Egyptians and their mummies.

J. D. Salinger told this story in his famous novel.

Forty years later, Adolfo Gilly was walking beside the lake in Central Park. There was no ice. It was an autumn day around noon, and a teacher was reading that very passage aloud.

His students were seated in a circle, listening.

Then a flock of ducks came swimming over. The ducks stayed there, hugging the shore, while the teacher carried on reading about them.

Afterward the teacher departed, followed by his students. As did the ducks.

# The River

Three centuries ago the river shook off the French. Later the English couldn't catch it either. It refused to stay put. Whenever an explorer mapped its course, the river would decamp that very night and flow elsewhere.

In 1830 the river was caught. The city of Chicago was nailed to its banks to keep it from ever fleeing again. Then at the end of the nineteenth century the city tamed it with walls of cement, forcing the water to flow backward.

One morning in the spring of 1992, after the river had behaved itself for a very long time, the city woke up to wet feet, a nasty surprise. The subway dripped, and basements did too. Having slipped its leash, the river was not to be stopped. It seeped through the walls first in drops, then spurts, then in a surging flood that drowned the streets.

After several days of rebellion the renegade was subdued.

To this day, the city sleeps with one eye open.

# Voices

Pedro Saad walked on the frozen waters of the Volga River. He was in the heart of Russia on a very cold winter afternoon. He was alone, but had company as he walked; he could feel through the thick soles of his boots the lively vibration of the river beneath the ice.

# The Flood

The streets were floral arrangements, the churches bonbon delights, the palaces gifts in a toy shop.

But beautiful Antigua, capital of Guatemala, lived with its heart in its mouth: the angry quaking earth condemned the city to perpetual anguish. What it didn't squander on tears, it spent on sighs.

In 1773 the land bucked like never before. The river leaped its banks, washing away people and houses. The flood's survivors had to flee and found another city far away.

The river that flooded was, and is, called Penastivo, Pensive.

# Snails

For assistance we turn to gods, devils, and the stars in the sky. We don't consult snails.

But thanks to snails the Shipibo Indians avoid drowning whenever the Ucayali River wakes up in a bad mood and rolls its white-capped waters inland over everything in its path.

Snails give warning. Before each calamity, they lay their eggs on tree trunks above the line where the water will crest. And they never get it wrong.

# The Deluge

Weary of so much disobedience and sin, God decided to wipe from the face of the earth the flesh he had created with his own hand. Humans and beasts and serpents and even the birds in the sky were to be obliterated.

When the sage Johannes Stoeffler announced the exact date of the second great flood, the fourth of February, 1524, Count von Igleheim simply shrugged. Then God himself came to him in his dreams, beard of lightning, voice of thunder, and declared, "You will drown."

Count von Igleheim, who knew the entire Bible by heart, leaped from his bed and called together the best carpenters in the region. Before you could say amen, an enormous ark, three stories tall, made of resinous wood and caulked inside and out, was floating on the Rhine. The count went on board with his family and all his servants and abundant supplies. He took along a male and female of every species of all the beasts of the land and the air. And he waited.

On the chosen day it rained. Not much, more like a drizzle, but the first drops were enough to spark panic and a crazed mass of people rushed the pier and swarmed over the ark.

The count tried to fight them off and was thrown into the river, where he drowned.

# Nets

On the sandbar at Guaratiba seagulls laugh raucously. The boats are unloading fish and fish stories.

One of the fishermen, Claudionor da Silva, scratches his head and sighs with regret. He'd managed to catch a good-sized porgy, but the fish pointed with his fin and said, "a bigger one's coming." Claudionor believed him and let him go.

Another, Jorge Antunes, is sporting new threads. He'd been lost at sea for several days when a huge wave carried off his drinking water and left him naked, he resigned himself to dying of sun and thirst. But then he managed to net a shark, and in the beast's belly he found an ice-cold can of Coke, a hat, a pair of pants, and a brand-new shirt.

Reinaldo Alves laughs with all his false teeth. Not to belittle such good fortune, he protests, but really I'm the lucky one. Far from the coast, he sneezed and his dentures flew overboard. He dove in after them and searched everywhere, but came up empty-handed. A couple of days later, he hauled in a flounder, and lo and behold the fish was wearing them.

# Shrimp

At the hour when the day bids adieu, fishermen on the Gulf of California prepare their nets.

When that old magician the sun casts its final glow, their canoes slide between the little islands that line the coast. There, they await the moon.

Shrimp spend the day hidden in the depths, hugging the mud or the sand. As soon as the moon comes out, the shrimp rise. Moonlight calls to them, and they answer. Then the fishermen take the nets folded on their shoulders and toss them. The nets open as they fall, broad wings in the air, and capture their prey.

Seeking the moon, the shrimp meet their doom.

From the looks of them, no one would imagine that these whiskery creatures harbored such a poetic bent. But from the taste of them, any human would swear to it.

# The Curse

She was born with the name of Langland, a three-masted iron-hulled schooner that carried saltpeter from Chile and guano from Peru over to Europe.

When she reached the age of twenty, her name was changed to María Madre, and her luck turned. She continued sailing across the sea, but misfortune pursued her and things went from bad to worse.

At the turn of the twentieth century, miserable from disrepair, the ship ran aground in the port of Paysandú and remained a prisoner there for the next forty years due to a mysterious and complicated legal battle over an unfulfilled contract.

In 1942, she was relaunched. And again she changed names. Now called Clara, she put to sea with a thousand tons of salt.

In a little while, as Clara was leaving the River Plate, a great cigar-shaped cloud rose over the horizon. A bad omen. The wind off the pampas bore down on the ship, smashed her to bits, and drove what was left of her ashore. Clara died on a beach called Las Delicias at the foot of a house. It was the summer home of Lorenzo Marcenaro, the very man who had baptized her the third time back on the dock at Paysandú.

Since then, no ship dares to change her name in these southern waters. The sea is free, but its daughters are not.

# The Sea

Rafael Alberti has been in the world for almost a century, yet today he contemplates the Bay of Cádiz as if for the first time.

Lying in the sun, he follows the unhurried paths of seagulls and sailboats, the azure breeze, the ebb and flow of foam on the water and in the air.

He turns to Marcos Ana, who sits silently at his side, and giving his friend's arm a squeeze he says, as if he has just found out, "Life is so short."

# Punishment

The city of Carthage was queen and master of the African coast. Her warriors reached the doors of Rome and came close to crushing the rival, the enemy, under the hoofs of their horses and the weight of their elephants.

A few years later, Rome took revenge. Carthage had to surrender her arms and warships and accept the humiliation of conquest and the obligation of tribute. Carthage hung her head in resignation. But when Rome ordered the people of Carthage to abandon the sea and move inland, far from the source of their arrogance and daring, they refused. Not that, never that. So Rome cursed Carthage and condemned her to death. The legions closed in.

Besieged from land and sea, for three years the city resisted. Not a speck of grain was left in the granaries; even the sacred monkeys of the temples had been devoured. Forgotten by her gods, inhabited only by ghosts, Carthage fell. For six days and six nights fires raged. Then Roman legionaries swept away the smoking ashes and sowed the land with salt, so that nothing and no one would ever flourish there again.

The city of Cartagena on the coast of Spain is the daughter of old Carthage, and the granddaughter is Cartagena de Indias, born much later on the shores of America. One night, in quiet conversation, Cartagena de Indias told me her secret: if some day they oblige her to move from the sea, she said, she too will choose death, just as her grandmother did.

# Another Punishment

Not only through banishment do coastal people lose their seas.

At the end of 2002 an oil tanker split in half and spewed its poison over Galicia and beyond. Day after day, a lethal sticky tide laid siege to the waters and the coast.

The blackened shoreline was a graveyard. Dead fish and dead birds floated in the putrid rot on the waters.

The authorities? Blind. The government? Deaf.

But the local fishermen, boats anchored, nets stowed, were not alone. Thousands upon thousands of volunteers stood with them to battle the enemy invasion. Armed with shovels and buckets and whatever they could find, day after day, week after week, they painstakingly stripped the sand and stones of their oily mourning garments.

Those many hands made no speeches. But they were not mute. By doing, they said, "Never again."

# Downpour

The sky parted and dumped its water, raining as if it intended to pour out every last drop, extending from one horizon to the other, and all that rain fell into the sea.

Over the whitecaps came a battleship. On deck, lying flat on his back, hands behind his head, a young soldier was letting himself be drenched. And asking himself questions.

Though he was in the service, science was his thing. He'd never seen the rain at sea, and he was trying to find an explanation for such a ridiculous phenomenon. As a good scientist, the soldier believed, or wanted to believe, that although Nature might act crazy and pretend to dementia, it always knows what it's doing.

Isaac Asimov spent hours and hours lying there, getting pelted with bullets from the sky, and he found no answer. Why would Nature pour water into the waterlogged sea, when so many thirsty places on Earth are begging the clouds for a little relief?

# Drought

Lamin Sennah and his brothers had stopped playing. Since the beginning of the drought, they'd done nothing but vainly scratch at the ground bombarded by the sun.

Their mother stripped her ears and neck, sold her jewelry and then her clothes and then the housewares.

Every day, at the center of the barren house, she lit a fire under the scrap swimming in the bottom of the pot.

They ate the last few kernels.

Their mother continued lighting the fire so the neighbors would see the smoke.

A long siege: hemmed in by drought, Lamin and his brothers spent their nights with their eyes open and their days yawning and shivering as if it were cold. Sitting around the fire, skinny arms around their knees, they no longer even begged the sky for rain.

Then their mother left and returned without the silver spoon she had always kept hidden under the floorboards.

The little spoon, her secret treasure, her only inheritance, had belonged to the grandparents of her grandparents, long before her country, Gambia, was a country.

That final sale provided them with a morsel.

"But the life went out of her," Lamin says.

Their mother never got up again. The fire at the center of the house went out.

# The Desert

When the world was still becoming the world, the mountain Tunupa lost her son. She got even by showering the earth with sour milk from her breasts and the Andean steppe turned into an infinite desert of salt.

The salt flats of Uyuni, born of that rage, swallows up travelers. Román Morales nonetheless set out across this place where llamas and vicuñas never venture.

He soon lost sight of the last signs of the world.

Hours passed, days, nights, while salt crystals crunched under his boots.

He wanted to turn back but didn't know how, and he wanted to go on but didn't know where. As much as he rubbed his eyes, he failed to see the horizon. Blinded by white light, he walked seeing nothing but the bright nothingness of glowing salt.

Every step hurt.

Román lost track of time.

Several times he collapsed. Each time he was kicked awake by the ice of the night or the fire of the day, and he got up and continued walking, with legs that were no longer his own.

When they found him, crumpled in a heap near the village of Altucha, the salt had long ago taken big bites from his boots and not a drop of water was left in his canteens.

Bit by bit he came back to life. And when he was sure that he was neither in Heaven nor in Hell, Román wondered, "Who was it that crossed the desert?"

# The Peasant

Angelo Giuseppe Roncalli, born and raised on a tiny plot of land, shed no tears of nostalgia when he recalled his childhood there.

"Men," he said, "have three ways of ruining their lives: women, gambling, and farming. Of the three, my father chose the most boring."

But every day he climbed the Tower of Wind, the Vatican's highest spire, and settled down to look. Spyglass in hand, he'd quickly scan the streets, then search for the seven hills on the outskirts of Rome where the land was still land. He'd spend hours contemplating the distant greenery, until duty obliged him to end his communion.

Then Angelo would put on his white cassock, and, with his pen in his pocket and his cross on his chest, the only things he owned in this world, he'd return to the throne where once again he'd become Pope John XXIII.

# Relatives

In 1992, while people were celebrating five centuries of something billed as the salvation of the Americas, a Catholic priest arrived at a community hidden in the ravines of the Mexican Southeast.

Before saying mass, he heard confession. In the Tojolobal language the Indians told their sins. Carlos Lenkersdorf translated as best he could, one confession after another, but he soon realized that no one could make sense of such mysteries.

"He says he abandoned his corn," Carlos translated. "He says the cornfield is very sad. Many days since he last went."

"He says he abused the fire. He cursed the flames, because they didn't glow brightly."

"He says he defiled the path, cutting back undergrowth when there was no need."

"He says he hurt the ox."

"He says he chopped down a tree, without telling it why."

The priest had no idea what to do with these sins that don't appear anywhere on Moses's list.

# Family

Jerónimo, José Saramago's grandfather, didn't know how to read or write, but he knew a great deal and what he knew he kept to himself.

When he fell ill, he knew that his time had come. He walked silently through his orchard, stopping beside each tree, and one by one he hugged them. He embraced the fig tree, the laurel, the pomegranate, and the three or four olive trees.

On the road, a car waited.

The car took him to Lisbon, to his death.

# The Offering

It was Enrique Castañares's birthday, and there was a party.

Nobody had invited Manuela Godoy, but the guitars called out to her.

She wasn't the sort to join in. She had lived and drunk away no one knew how many years, but with no one, for no one, always keeping to her shack on the outskirts of the town of Robles. People knew only that she was so poor she had nothing, not even fleas, and so lonely she slept with her arms around a bottle.

But the night of the party, Manuela hung about the Castañares house, peering in the windows, until they asked her in and she joined the dancing throng.

She wore everyone out, dancing to every song and drinking all the wine.

She was the last to leave. They wrapped up what was left of the barbecue and a few empanadas, and with them bundled into a sack she headed off at the end of the night. Weaving from side to side, she entered the cornfield and vanished.

The following morning, when Enrique looked out the door, she was standing there, waiting. "What did you forget, Doña Manuela?"

She shook her head. In her hands, as if in a chalice, glowed a squash. It was the first harvest from her garden. "For you," she said.

# Grapes

Those weren't fireworks, they were the sounds of war.

Over Zagreb, shells and bombs jolted a sky lit up by tracer bullets.

The old year was dying, and Yugoslavia was dying too, while Fran Sevilla filed his final story of the year for Radio Nacional in Madrid.

Fran hung up the phone and flicked his cigarette lighter to see his watch. He ran his tongue over his lips, swallowed. He was alone in an empty hotel, accompanied only by the screams of sirens and the thunder of bombs, and the new year was just a few minutes away. Flashes from the explosions were the only light in the room.

Lying in bed, Fran pulled twelve grapes from a bunch. At midnight, on the dot, he ate them.

With each grape, one by one, he tapped with a fork on a bottle of Rioja he had brought from Spain.

Clinking the bottle was something Fran learned as a child from his father, when they lived on the outskirts of Madrid in a neighborhood that had no church bells.

# Wine

Lucila Escudero didn't act her age.

Though she had buried seven children, she still looked at the world with the eyes of a newborn. She puttered around her three gardens in Santiago, Chile, three tiny jungles she watered every day. After chatting with her plants, she'd set off to explore the neighborhood, deaf to her own sorrows and sufferings and to all the sad voices of time.

Lucila believed in Paradise and knew that she deserved it, but she felt much better at home. To put death off the scent, she slept in a different spot every night. Some great-grandchild was always available to help her move the bed, and she grinned ear to ear imagining the Grim Reaper's rage when he came for her.

Then she'd light her last cigarette of the day, in her long, carved cigarette holder, fill a glass with Maipo Valley red, and glide into dreamland with her Our Fathers and Ave Marias and a sip for every amen.

# The Wine Bar

We called it The Webs, after the output of the spider Ramona, who wove endlessly on the ceiling, setting a fine example for the working class in the port of Montevideo.

A greengrocer's by day, the place became a wine shop by night. Under the stars, we nighthawks drank and sang and talked.

The running tabs were kept on the wall behind the counter.

"That wall's so dirty it's going to collapse," customers would say, now and then, between drinks.

The D'Alessandro brothers, Lito and Rafa, one roly-poly and the other gaunt, turned a deaf ear until they ran out of room for more numbers.

Then came the Night of Forgiveness, when whitewash cleared the accounts.

The regulars celebrated the occasion, baptizing new customers with a clink of a wineglass to the forehead.

# Beer

The elixir leads to ruin. To the ruin of slugs.

At nightfall they emerge from their hiding places and at a slug's pace march off to dine on the green flesh of plants.

In the middle of the garden, a glass of beer keeps watch. The temptation is irresistible. Drawn by the aroma, the slugs climb the side of the glass. From the edge of the abyss, they contemplate the tasty foam, and then, forgoing all caution, down they slide. In the sea of beer, drunk and happy, they drown.

# Forbidden Fruit

Dámaso Rodríguez had cows but no pasture. His cows wandered everywhere, and the moment he got distracted, they'd set out for the town of Ureña, for the park of their temptation.

They'd go straight to the big mango grove, where the trees stood swollen with fruit and a carpet of mangos covered the ground.

The police would interrupt their banquet. They'd drive the cows out with their nightsticks and lock them up.

Dámaso spent hours in the station house, putting up with the long wait and the longer lecture, until at last he could pay the fine and free his cows.

Aura, his daughter, sometimes went with him. She'd be all teary-eyed, while her father explained that the officers knew what they were doing. Even though there were plenty of mangos and they'd just wither on the ground, animals don't deserve such a feast. Cows are not worthy of the golden nectar, reserved for men as solace for living.

"Don't cry, my dear. Police are police, cows are cows, and men are men," Dámaso said.

Aura, who was neither police, nor a cow, nor a man, squeezed his hand.

# Carnal Sin

He made the count as usual. His men didn't know how it had happened, or they were lying. He counted again, made sure. A calf was missing.

He caught the hired hand he suspected, secured him with rope, mounted his horse, and dragged him off.

The man was more dead than alive, his flesh torn by the rocky ground, but Don Carmen Itriago still took his time and pinned him with great care. He drove in stakes one after the other, and with moist rawhide he tied down the condemned man's hands, feet, waist, and neck.

What remained of the man cried out, "I'll pay for the calf, Don Carmen. I'll give you whatever you say. I'll give you my life."

"At last, an offer I can't refuse," the boss said from high up on his horse, and he trotted off through the dust.

There were no witnesses, except for the horse, who by now is dead. Of the hired hand, eaten by the ants and the sun, not even his name is left. Only his bones, arms spread like a crucifix on the red earth. And Don Carmen wasn't the sort of man to talk about such things, because private property is part of private life, and that's nobody's business.

Nevertheless, Alfredo Armas Alfonzo told the story. He was there without being there, and he saw without seeing, the way he has seen everything that has happened since the world became the world in this wide valley split by the Unare River.

# Carnal Hunt

Arnaldo Bueso turned fifteen.

His elders celebrated the birthday with a great hunt in the woods on the banks of the Ajagual River. It being his first hunt, they assigned him a place in the rear and left him in a dense thicket with instructions not to move. There he lay, gazing at the .22 that gazed back at him, while the hunters loosed their dogs and set off at top speed.

The barking faded into the distance; the sounds slowly ebbed away.

The rifle remained, hanging from a long belt tied to the branch of a tree.

Arnaldo did not dare touch it. Flat on his back, hands behind his head, he entertained himself watching the birds flutter about in the leaves. The wait was long. Lulled by birdsong, he fell asleep.

The crash of breaking branches jerked him awake. Paralyzed with fear, he managed to make out an enormous deer stampeding toward him. The deer jumped, got snagged in the rifle belt, and Arnaldo heard a shot. The animal fell dead.

The entire town of Santa Rosa de Copán celebrated the unrivaled triumph: a sure shot from below, mid-leap, straight to the heart.

At home with friends some years later, Arnaldo interrupted an animated round of drinks. He asked for silence, as if about to give a speech. Pointing to the enormous antlers that bore witness to his first and final hunting glory, he confessed, "It was suicide."

# Carnal Affront

A man imprisoned by desire walked alone in the elements. The soft hills of the countryside not far from Montevideo swelled into disturbing curves of breasts and thighs. Paco gazed upward, seeking escape from temptation, but the sky denied his eyes the peace they sought: the clouds moved in step, swaying as one, offering themselves to each other.

Paco's sister Victoria, who owned the farm, had warned him: "Absolutely not. No chicken stew. Don't touch the chickens."

But Paco Espínola had studied the Greeks and knew something about the question of fate. His legs urged him toward forbidden territory, and, obedient to the voice of destiny, he went along.

Much later, Victoria watched him approach. Paco walked slowly, and he carried something dangling from his hand. When Victoria realized it was a dead chicken, she turned into a fury.

Paco called for silence. And he told the truth.

He'd entered the coop in search of shade and saw a red-feathered hen. He gave it a few kernels of corn, the hen ate them and said, "Thank you."

Then another hen, the color of snow, just as polite, came over to eat and also said, "Thank you."

"But then this one came along," Paco said, swinging the bird from its wrung neck. "I offered her a few kernels. She wouldn't touch them. 'Won't you eat, sweetie?' I asked. And she raised her crest and said, 'Go fuck your mother.' Can you imagine, Victoria? Our mother? Our mother!"

# Diet

Sarah Tarler Bergholz was very short. She didn't have to sit down for her grandchildren to comb her hair, which fell in tight curls from her pretty face to her belly button.

Sarah was so fat that she couldn't breathe. In a Chicago hospital the doctor told her the obvious: to bring her height and weight back to proportion, she had to follow a strict diet, avoiding all fat.

She had a voice of silk. Her brashest statements sounded like intimate confessions. As if sharing a secret, she fixed her eyes on the doctor and said, "I'm not sure life is worth living without salami."

The following year, embracing her undoing, she died. Her heart failed. To science, the cause was no mystery; but we'll never really know whether her heart tired of eating salami or of giving.

# Food

Nicolasa's aunt taught her how to walk and how to cook.

Beside the wood stove, her aunt revealed the secrets of dishes that, through inheritance or invention, would emerge from her hand. That's how Nicolasa discovered the ancient mysteries of the Mexican table, and learned to celebrate astonishing marriages of savory flavors to piquant spices that had never before had the pleasure of meeting.

Soon after the aunt died, complaints started pouring in from the cemetery. The racket coming from her grave was so bad that the dead couldn't sleep. Until someone made use of her recipes, she was not going to rest in peace.

Nicolasa had no choice but to open a little place. Where she sells meals to go that would delight the gods, if only the unfortunate gods didn't live so far away.

# Unstill Life

Alfredo Mires Ortiz wanted to compile a list of the customs and seasons of Cajamarca. The local people suggested a few categories:

eclipse
rain
flood
mist
frost
gust
whirlwind

Alfredo agreed. "Oh, yes," he said. "Natural phenomena."
With time, Alfredo learned.
The eclipse happens, he learned, because the sun and the moon can't get along, sun of fire, moon of water. The couple is so quarrelsome that when they meet up, the sun either burns the moon or the moon douses the sun.
The rain, he learned, is the sister of the rivers.
That the earth's blood runs through the rivers, and that flooding results when blood is spilled.
That the mist has a fine time playing tricks on people out walking.
That frost is one-eyed, which is why it burns the crops only on one side.
That the gust licks its lips eating seeds planted under a new moon.
And that the whirlwind spins because it has only one foot.

# Soul in Plain Sight

According to an ancient belief, the tree of life grows upside down. Its leaves burrow into the earth, its roots gaze at the sky. It offers not its fruits but its origins. Rather than hiding underground what is most intimate, most vulnerable, it bares its roots, exposing them to the winds of the world.

"That's life," says the tree of life.

# The Ginkgo

It is the oldest of all trees, around since the dinosaurs.

They say its leaves prevent asthma, cure headaches, and relieve the discomforts of old age.

They also say that ginkgo is the best remedy for poor memory. This claim has been proven. When the atom bomb turned the city of Hiroshima into a blackened wasteland, an old ginkgo was leveled near the epicenter of the explosion. The tree was burned to cinders, just like the Buddhist temple it protected. Three years later, someone found a little green shoot peeking out from the charcoal. The dead stump had sprouted. The tree revived, opened its arms, flowered.

The survivor of the massacre is still there.

So people will know.

# Living History

As they tell it in Veracruz, this house was Hernán Cortés's first home in the land of Mexico.

Cortés ordered it made of adobe, with stones from the Huitzilapan River and coral from the reefs offshore near a place where he'd anchored his flagship.

The house still stands and looks alive even though it died of suffocation. An enormous tree with a thousand arms strangled the house of the quistador. Branches, vines, and roots shattered the walls, invaded the patio, and smothered the windows, barring the smallest flicker of light. The dense foliage left one door open, for no one. Day after day, the tree proceeds with its leisurely ritual of devouring the work of centuries, under the indifferent or scornful eye of the neighbors.

# The Cuxín

There she was born, there she took her first steps.

When Rigoberta returned, years later, her village was gone. Soldiers had left nothing alive in what had been called Laj Chimel, little Chimel, the place you could hold in the palm of your hand. They killed the people and the corn and the hens; the few Indians who managed to escape into the dense forest had to strangle the dogs so their barking wouldn't give them away.

Rigoberta Menchú wandered through the mist, uphill and down, in search of the creeks of her childhood, but there were none. The waters where she once bathed had gone dry, or perhaps they'd just gone, far away.

Of the oldest trees, which she'd believed would stand forever, only rotten stumps remained. Their powerful branches had served as gallows, their trunks as backdrops for the firing squads; afterward the trees let themselves die.

Through the mist, into the mist Rigoberta walked, drop with no bud with no branch. She searched for her dear friend the cuxín and found only dry, exposed roots. Nothing else was left of the tree that during her years of exile used to visit her in dreams, covered with white, yellow-hearted blossoms.

The cuxín had aged overnight and pulled itself out by the roots.

# The Tree Remembers

Seven women sat in a circle.

From far away, from the town of Momostenango, Humberto Ak'abal brought them a few dry leaves he'd collected at the foot of a Spanish cedar.

Each woman crushed a leaf, quietly, next to her ear. And each opened a window on the tree's memory:

One felt the wind blowing.

Another, the branch swaying softly.

A third, the beating of a bird's wings.

Yet another heard rain falling.

One, the scurrying of a beetle.

Another, the echo of voices.

The last, the low murmur of footsteps.

# The Flower Remembers

It looks like an orchid, but it's not. It smells like a gardenia, but it's not that either. Its large petals tremble like white wings yearning to fly away and leave the stalk behind. That must be why in Cuba they call it *mariposa,* "butterfly."

Alessandra Riccio planted a butterfly bulb she brought from Havana to Naples. In the strange earth of a far-off land, the butterfly came into leaf but did not flower. Months and years went by, and it sprouted nothing but greenery.

Until a few of Alessandra's Cuban friends came to visit and spent a week at her house. The plant was surrounded by the lilting sounds of home, that melodious Caribbean way of singing the words they speak. For seven days and seven nights, the plant listened to the music of conversation, since Cubans talk whenever they're awake and also in their sleep.

After bidding her friends good-bye at the airport, Alessandra returned home to find the white petals of a newborn flower.

# The Jacaranda

By night, Norberto Paso hefted cargo in the port of Buenos Aires.

By day, far from the port, he built this house. Blanca brought him bricks and buckets of mortar, and the walls rose up around the dirt yard.

The house was half finished when Blanca brought home a jacaranda. It was a small tree, costing a small fortune. Norberto shook his head. "You're nuts," he said, and helped her plant it.

When they finished the house, Blanca died.

Years have passed, and now Norberto rarely goes out. Once a week he travels several hours to join other old men in the city center and protest because their pensions are crap that wouldn't even buy enough rope to hang themselves with.

When Norberto returns late at night, the jacaranda is there, waiting for him.

# The Plane Tree

His teacher died an infamous death on a cross in Jerusalem.

Twenty centuries later, bullets split open Carlos Mugica's chest on a street in Buenos Aires.

Orlando Yorio, his brother in the faith, wanted to clean up Carlos's blood. He brought a bucket of water and a mop, but the police wouldn't let him. So Orlando stood in front of the house, mop in hand, his gaze fixed on the puddle big enough to be the blood of many.

Suddenly, without warning, a furious downpour washed the blood toward the foot of a plane tree. The tree drank it to the last drop.

# Green Dialogue

They look stationary, but they breathe and move, seeking the light.

And they talk. Few people know this, but when a tree gets cut or bruised, it protects itself by secreting poison, and it sends out an alarm to other trees. Words travel through the air that in tree language say, "danger" and "watch out." Then the other trees protect themselves by secreting poison too.

Maybe that's how it's been since trees first stood tall and multiplied, when the forests were so vast that it's said a squirrel could circle the earth hopping from branch to branch.

Now, between one desert and the next, the surviving trees keep alive their ancient custom of taking care of each other.

# Mute

Many are the rings inscribed on their trunks. These giant trees, heavy with years, have spent centuries chained to the depths of the earth, and they cannot escape. Defenseless against chain saws, they crack and fall. Whenever one topples, a world comes crashing down, and flocks of birds are left homeless.

Unwieldy old trees are fated to die. In their place grow profitable young saplings. Native forests give way to contrived forests. Order—military, industrial—triumphs over the chaos of nature. Pine and eucalyptus grown for export look like soldiers in formation, marching off to the world market.

Fast food, fast wood. Man-made forests grow overnight and are sold in the time it takes to say amen. Source of hard currency, triumph of development, symbol of progress, these wood farms suck the land dry and leave the soil barren.

No birds sing in them.

People call them "forests of silence."

# Alone

The macaw was but a chick in a nest when his tree was felled.

Imprisoned in a birdcage, he spent his whole life indoors. When his owner died, he was abandoned. The Schlenkers, who run a refuge for lost animals near Quito, took him in.

The macaw had never laid eyes on a relative. Now he can't get along with other macaws or with any of his parrot cousins.

He can't even get along with himself. Hunched in a corner, he shakes and screeches, pecks and pulls out his feathers, until his plucked skin bleeds.

Poor thing, I say. Nothing could be lonelier. But then Abdón Ubidia, who brought me to the refuge, introduces me to the loneliest creature in the world.

It is the last aguti paca, or wild guinea pig. He spends his nights walking in circles and his days hidden in the hollow trunk of a fallen tree. In this region, he is the only one of his species left alive. All of his kind have been exterminated.

While he awaits death, he has not a soul to talk to.

# Houdini

His captors cut off one wing when they took him in the jungle. Kitty Hischier found him in the Puerto Vallarta market. She felt sorry for him and bought him thinking she'd set him free. But the parrot couldn't manage on his own. In his mutilated state, he'd have been an easy snack for the first hungry gullet to come along. Kitty decided to sneak him across the border in her pickup. He would join the thousands upon thousands of other undocumented Mexicans in the United States.

She called him Houdini, because he kept trying to escape. The first day on the road he raised the cage door with his powerful beak. The second day he pulled up the cage floor. The third day he made a hole in the wire screening. On the fourth, he tried to flee through the roof, but he no longer had the strength.

Houdini wouldn't eat or utter a sound. On hunger strike and in mutinous silence, he died.

# Frogs

They say a girl's kiss will turn a frog into a prince. Frogs don't seem all that kissable, but there are girls who have tried. It hasn't worked.

But when pesticides kiss a frog, it turns into a monster.

In the past, little frogs rarely turned out deformed. But the rare has become commonplace in the lakes of Minnesota, the woods of Pennsylvania, and elsewhere. Fewer and fewer frogs develop at all, and more and more emerge without eyes or with an extra leg or one leg missing.

By the time frogs had their fatal date with chemicals, they'd lived between water and land for millions of years, beginning on the remote day when the song of the first frog broke the world's silence.

# Seeds

In Brazil, peasant farmers asked, Why are there so many people without land when there is so much land without people? The answer came by bullet.

Fear was their only inheritance, and they lost it. They kept on asking questions and taking land and committing the crime of wanting to work.

In their millions they asked, Why are chemicals allowed to torture the earth? What will happen to us if seeds are no longer seeds?

At the beginning of 2001 landless peasants invaded an experimental plot planted with genetically modified seeds belonging to the Monsanto corporation in Rio Grande do Sul. They left not one artificial soy plant standing.

The plantation was called Não me toque—"Do Not Touch."

# Herbs

For heartburn, tomatoes peeled and grilled.

For indigestion, boiled leaves of *tepozán*.

For muscle aches, ointments of maguey, India rubber, or cooked cactus pears.

Cactus flesh and sarsparilla purified the blood, pea pods cleansed the kidneys, and pine nuts purged the intestines.

Five-fingered flowers from the tree of little hands gave the heart serenity and courage.

The conquistadores found these novelties in Mexico. They carried them back to Spain, along with other herbs with unpronounceable Indian names that relieved fever, killed parasites, soothed the urinary tract, countered the poison of snake bites.

Ancient American pharmacology was well received in Europe.

A few years later the Holy Inquisition unleashed its dogs. Knowledge of plants was a tool of witches and demons disguised as doctors, who deserved the rack or the stake. Beneath their exotic robes lay the cloven hoof of the Malignant one.

Brews and unguents from America came from Hell, as did the fires of chocolate and the smoke of tobacco, which incited sinning in another's bed. Likewise, the devilish mushrooms pagans ate to float in the air by the cunning evil of their idolatries.

# The Lady Who Heals

Is this mountain really a mountain?

Or is it a woman—monumental breasts, curved knees—lying in the sun?

In the Navajo language, her name is Diichiti.

Clouds shower her body, from which sprout herbs that offer cures or consolation.

Her insides are made of pumice. The company Arizona Tufflite has nibbled away at her for years, laying bare her raw flesh. Not much is left of her green skin. The great wounds are visible for miles.

The pace of excavation has picked up since fashion deemed the new must look old and jeans worn soft by pumice became all the rage. But so has the pace of protest, and this time the many voices became a single thunderclap. United were the Navajo, Hopi, Hualapai, Diné, Zuni, and other peoples forever divided by those who rule over them. And the company had to depart.

As the new millennium commenced, the Indians began to heal the lady who heals them.

# The Lady Who Listens

At the same time, thousands of leagues to the south, bullets chased the U'wa Indians off their land in the mountains of Samoré.

Helicopters and ground troops cleared the way for Occidental Petroleum, and the Colombian press hailed "this advance party of progress in a hostile environment."

When the drills set to work, experts declared the wells would produce no fewer than four hundred million barrels of oil.

Every day at dawn and dusk, the Indians gathered on the misty peaks to chant their incantations.

After a year the company had spent sixty million dollars and had found not a drop of oil.

The U'wa proved once more that the earth is not deaf. She heard their pleas and hid the oil, her black blood, so the trees would not die, the grass would not wither, the springs would not be poisoned.

In their language, *U'wa* means "People who think."

# The Gentleman Who Speaks

Not long ago in the Valley of Mexico, a mountain erupted.

Clouds of flame, rocks on fire, blistering ash: Popocatépetl vomited the stones that had stopped up its mouth, which was as wide as four soccer fields.

Evacuating the nearby towns was almost impossible.

"No," people said. "He is good. He won't harm us."

The locals have always eaten and drunk with Don Popo. They offer him tortillas, tequila, and music, and they ask him for rain for the beans and corn and for protection against hail and evil winds in the air and in life. He answers through the mouths of the masters of time, who listen to him while they dream and then recount his words.

That's the custom. But this time Popo gave no warning. The masters of time did not know that the volcano was choking, that it had had enough of talking through other mouths.

The volcano spoke his piece.

He killed no one.

In one town on the slopes, three weddings took place on the night of the eruption, as if nothing were amiss. The red glow from above lit up the ceremonies.

# The Gentleman Who Remains Silent

In colonial times, Cerro Rico in Potosí produced much silver and many widows.

For over two centuries in the freezing heights of South America, Europe observed a Western Christian ritual: day after day, night after night, Europe fed the mountain human flesh in exchange for silver.

For every ten Indians who entered the mouths of the shafts, seven never came out. The killings occurred in Bolivia, which did not yet have that name, so that the dawn of capitalism, which also did not yet have that name, could occur in Europe.

Today, Cerro Rico is hollow, his silver long gone.

In the Indians' language, *Potosí*, or *Potojsi*, means " to thunder" or "to explode." Tradition has it that the mountain would thunder when wounded. Now emptied, he remains silent.

# First Lessons

From moles we learned to make tunnels.
From beavers we learned to make dams.
From birds we learned to build homes.
From spiders we learned to weave.
From tree trunks rolling downhill we learned about wheels.
From tree trunks floating and adrift we learned about boats.
From wind we learned about sails.
How did we learn our evil ways? From whom did we learn to torment our neighbors and subdue the earth?

# Judgment Day

I can't get the feeling out of my head that at some point we'll all face Judgment Day. I imagine being interrogated by prosecutors who point their fins or branches, accusing us of turning the kingdom of this world into a desert of stone. "What have you done to the planet? Did you think you'd bought it at the supermarket? Who gave you the right to kill us?"

I see a high tribunal of flora and fauna handing down the sentence, eternal damnation, to the human species.

Will the innocent pay as well as the guilty? Will we all spend eternity in Hell, roasting on a slow fire alongside the fat cats who actually poisoned the earth, the water, and the air?

I used to think Judgment Day was God's business: black sun, blood moon, divine rage. If worst came to worst, I'd have to share an interminable barbecue with serial killers, TV stars, and book critics.

Now, by comparison, that seems like nothing.

# Map of Time

Some four and a half billion years ago, give or take a year, a dwarf star spit out a planet now called Earth.

Some four billion two hundred million years ago, the first cell took a sip of sea broth and liked it. Then the first cell divided in two, so it would have someone to offer a drink.

Some four million years ago and a bit, woman and man, all but apes, rose up on their legs and embraced, and for the first time experienced the joy and panic of looking into each other's eyes while doing so.

Some four hundred fifty thousand years ago, woman and man struck two stones together and lit the first fire, which helped them battle fear and cold.

Some three hundred thousand years ago, woman and man spoke the first words and believed they understood each other.

And there we are still: wanting to be two, dying of fear, dying of cold, searching for words.

# Silence

A long table of friends in a restaurant called Plataforma was Tom Jobim's refuge from the noonday sun and the noisy streets of Rio de Janeiro.

One day, Tom sat in the corner drinking beer with Zé Fernando Balbi. The two shared a straw hat which they wore by turns, Tom one day, Zé Fernando the next, and they shared a few other things as well.

"No," said Tom, when someone came by, "I'm in the middle of an important conversation."

And when another friend approached: "You'll have to excuse me, but we have a lot to talk about."

Once more: "Sorry, but we're discussing a serious matter."

Off in their corner, Tom and Zé Fernando said not a word. Zé Fernando was having one of those rotten days that ought to be crossed off the calendar and erased from memory, and Tom was keeping him company with silent beers. They stayed that way, immersed in the music of silence, from noon till dusk.

The restaurant was empty when they got up and ambled to the door.

# The Word

In the jungle of the Upper Paraná, a trucker warned me to be careful. "Keep your eye out for savages," he said. "There are still a few on the loose."

He told me this in Spanish. But that wasn't his language. The trucker spoke Guaraní, the tongue of the savages he feared and scorned.

Strange thing: Paraguay speaks the language of the vanquished. And stranger still: the vanquished believe and continue to believe that words are sacred. A lie insults whatever it names, but truth reveals its soul. The vanquished believe the soul resides in the words it speaks. If I give my word, I give myself. The tongue is not a garbage dump.

# The Letter

Enrique Buenaventura was drinking rum in a Cali bar when a stranger approached his table. The man introduced himself as a bricklayer, please forgive the disrespect, pardon the intrusion. "I need you to write a letter for me. A love letter."

"Me?"

"I was told you can do it."

Enrique was no expert but his heart swelled. The bricklayer explained that he was not illiterate. "I can write. But not that kind of letter."

"Who is the letter for?"

"For . . . her."

"And what do you want to tell her?"

"If I knew, I wouldn't be asking you."

Enrique scratched his head.

That night he got down to work.

The next day the bricklayer read the letter. "This," he said, and his eyes shone, "this is it. But until now I didn't know that this was what I wanted to say."

# The Letters

Juan Ramón Jiménez opened the envelope on his bed in the sanatorium on the outskirts of Madrid.

He looked at the letter, admired the photograph. "Thanks to your poems, I am no longer alone. I think of you so often!" confessed Georgina Hübner, his unknown admirer writing to him from afar. The pink paper of that first letter smelled of roses, and the picture of a smiling lady in a rocking chair in a Lima rose garden was tinted with rosaniline.

The poet wrote back. Sometime later a ship carried another letter from Georgina to Spain. She reproached him for his ceremonious language. Juan Ramón's apology journeyed to Peru. "Pardon me if I sounded formal, believe me when I point to my old enemy shyness." One letter followed another, traveling slowly between north and south, between the sick poet and his impassioned reader.

When Juan Ramón was released and returned to his home in Andalusia, the first thing he did was to send Georgina a heartfelt expression of his gratitude. And she answered with words that made his hands tremble.

Georgina's letters were a collective effort. A group of friends wrote them from a bar in Lima. It was all made up: the photograph, the name, the letters, the delicate handwriting. Every time something came from Juan Ramón, the friends got together, considered how to reply, and set to writing.

With time and the to-ing and fro-ing of letters, things began to change. They planned one letter and ended up writing another, much less constrained, inspired, perhaps dictated by their collective daughter, who was nothing like any of them and would bow to none of them.

Then came the letter announcing Juan Ramón's trip. The poet was coming to Lima, to the woman who had restored him to health and happiness.

An emergency meeting. What to do? Confess? How to inflict such cruelty? They debated long and hard and they made up their minds.

The next day, the Peruvian consul in Andalusia knocked at Juan Ramón's door amid the olive trees of Moguer. The consul had received an urgent telegram from Lima: "Georgina Hübner is dead."

# The Mailman

I saw him in the casket, wearing that unruffled, mischievous expression on his face and I thought: It can't be. Chubby Soriano is just pretending.

Confirmation came from his son Manuel, who looked just like Chubby, only smaller. He told me he'd given his father a letter to take to Filipi, a friend who had died a few days earlier.

Filipi was a lizard. A strange lizard who acted like a chameleon, changing color whenever he felt like it. In the letter, Manuel taught him a game so Filipi could amuse himself while he was dead, because being dead is really boring. To play the game, you had to write something in capital letters. "Use your claws, Filipi," Manuel told him.

So that was what had happened. Osvaldo Soriano, whose life had been spent writing stories and novels, letters to his readers, was now delivering the mail. He'd be back soon.

# The Reader

In one of his stories, Soriano imagined a soccer game in some little town lost in Patagonia. No one had ever managed to put one in the net against the local team at home. That kind of insult would have met with a hanging or fatal beating. In the story, the visiting team resisted temptation for the entire match, but in the closing minutes the center striker ended up alone, facing the goalkeeper, and had no choice but to send the ball between his legs.

Ten years later, when Soriano landed at the Neuquén airport, a stranger gripped him in a hug that raised him off the ground, suitcase and all.

"It wasn't just any goal, it was incredible!" he screamed. "I can see you right now! You rejoiced like Pelé!" And the man fell to his knees, lifting his arms to the heavens.

Then he covered his head. "Talk about raining stones! What a thrashing they gave us!"

His mouth open, suitcase in hand, Soriano listened.

"They were all over you! The whole town!" the maniac yelled. And indicating Soriano with his thumb, he told the gathering onlookers, "I saved this guy's life."

Then he proceeded to recount, in minute detail, the tremendous brawl that broke out at the end of the match Soriano had played, alone, one far-off night, sitting with his typewriter, a couple of sleepy cats, and an ashtray filled with butts.

# The Book

Reina Reyes wanted Felisberto Hernández to be free to devote himself to writing his wonderful stories and playing the piano. Writing earned him few readers and not a cent, and music was no money-maker either. Felisberto traveled deep into Uruguay and along the Argentina coast giving concerts, and he always had to leave his hotel by the window.

Reina was a teacher, she worked hard to make a living. In all the years he lived with her, Felisberto never heard her speak of money.

The first of every month, Reina gave him a book by one of the novelists or poets he liked. The book contained the freedom that delivered him from the hell of office work or the torment of other employment that steals hours and squanders life. Every few pages, he would find a bill, ironed flat.

# The Ink

The chroniclers of the conquest of America outdid themselves praising the rare fruit, never before seen or tasted, that Mexican Indians called *ahuacátl* and Peruvians *palta*.

They wrote that it was shaped like a pear and looked like the breast of a fair damsel. That it grew untended in the forest, with God as its gardener. That its delicate flesh, neither sweet nor sour, buttered the mouth, restored the sick, and roused the lazy. And nothing better kindled the fires of love.

The fruit, meanwhile, took these homages as its due, and to keep them from fading she offered the indelible ink of her seeds. The praise was written in avocado ink.

# Alphabet Soup

In size and sheen, he resembles a teardrop. Scientists call him *Lepisma saccharina,* but he answers to the name silverfish, even though he's no fish and has never seen the sea.

His speciality is devouring books, though he's no worm either. He'll eat whatever he finds, novels, poetry, encyclopedias, swallowing word after word in any language at his leisure.

He spends his entire life in the dim light of libraries. Of everything else he's oblivious. Daylight would kill him.

He would be quite the scholar, if he weren't an insect.

# She Tells

Chiti Hernández-Martí sat on a bench under the leafy canopy of Retiro Park and breathed deeply of the green air. She closed her eyes.

When she opened them, a dwarf was at her side.

He introduced himself as a toreador. She imagined the size of the bull and frowned.

"You look sad," the dwarf said. And he asked, no—demanded, "Tell me about it."

She shook her head, but the dwarf insisted. "Trust me, Snow White."

And Chiti murmured the first man's name that came into her head, while thinking how tough the life of a dwarf bullfighter must be. Then she said, making it up, "That creep made a fool of me."

As the story grew into a novel about a jerk who beat her, abused her, called her a worthless whore, Chiti felt less and less pity for the dwarf and only more for herself, by then pregnant by that two-faced bum of a married man with kids of his own. "How could I have done this to my boyfriend, who's so good? The poor angel doesn't deserve this, and now my mother's thrown me out and I've lost my job and I don't know what will become of me, I don't know my way around this city, I have nobody, they all slam the door in my face . . ."

The dwarf, overwhelmed, gazed silently at his feet dangling in the air. Chiti shivered even though it was midsummer, while a stream of real tears flowed from her eyes through the park and toward the pond where rowboats bob on the water.

# He Tells

It was the time of exile. Far from his country, Héctor Tizón's longing for home cut deep and left him raw.

Someone recommended therapy, but he and the psychoanalyst spent each eternal session in silence. The patient lying on the couch said nothing because he was taciturn by nature and in any case thought his life story utterly unimportant. The therapist said nothing either, and session after session the blank pages of the notebook on his knees remained untouched. After fifty minutes the psychoanalyst would sigh and say, "Okay. Time's up."

Héctor felt sorry for the doctor and sorry for himself.

He decided things couldn't stay that way.

From then on, while the midmorning train took him from Cercedilla to Madrid, Héctor made up stories. As soon as he touched the couch, he swung away on a rainbow and began to spin stories of mountains bewitched, souls whistling in the night, evil lights in the mist, and mermaids strumming guitars on the banks of the Yala River.

# The Shipwreck

Albert Londres traveled a lot and wrote a lot. He wrote about the boiling fury of the Balkans and Algeria, the trenches of the First World War, the barricades of Russia and China, the black slave trade in Dakar and the white slave trade in Buenos Aires, the poverty of pearl fishers in Aden, and the hell of prisoners in Cayenne.

On a calm night, while he walked the streets of Shanghai, something like a shaft of lightning struck him with the terrible force of revelation.

Some god, I suppose, did him a favor, out of courtesy or cruelty.

From then on, he couldn't eat or sleep.

He devoted every waking and dreaming hour to a book he considered his first, although he already had over twenty in print. Holed up in his hotel room by the docks, he set to work, then carried on, still feverish, in his cabin on the *Georges Phillipar*.

When it reached the Red Sea, the ship caught fire. Albert had to come on deck, where he was pushed and shoved into a lifeboat. A short distance from the wreck, Albert smacked his forehead, screamed "My book!" and jumped overboard. He swam to the burning ship, somehow clambered on board, and dashed into the flames, where his book was ablaze.

Neither of them were ever heard of again.

# Praise for the Press

Alberto Villagra was a glutton for the papers. At breakfast, hot off the griddle, the news rustled in his hands.

One morning he vowed, "Someday I'll read the paper riding an elephant."

His wife, Rosita, was game. They scrimped and saved until they could travel to India. Alberto didn't have breakfast on the back of the elephant, but he managed to read a Bombay paper without falling off.

Helena, his daughter, is also a newspaper addict. Her first cup of coffee has no aroma, flavor, or meaning if it doesn't come with the paper. And if the paper is missing, the first symptoms of withdrawal set in—trembles, nausea, stuttering.

Helena doesn't want flowers on her grave. Her will specifies, "Bring me the paper."

# Instructions for Reading the Paper

General Francisco Serrano of Mexico was settled in an easy chair at the Sonora army casino, smoking and reading.

He was reading the news. The paper was upside down.

President Álvaro Obregón was curious. "Do you always read the paper upside down?"

The general nodded.

"And could I ask why?"

"From experience, Mr. President, from experience."

# Instructions for a Successful Career

A thousand years ago, the sultan of Persia said, "How delicious."

He was eating his first eggplant, sliced and dressed with ginger and Nile herbs.

The court poet praised the eggplant for the pleasure it brings to the palate and the bedroom, for the miraculous feats of love that outshine the wonders of powdered tiger's tooth or grated rhinoceros horn.

Mouthfuls later, the sultan said, "What garbage."

The court poet then cursed the perfidious eggplant for the torments it wreaks on stomach and brain, for the delirium and insanity that brings virtuous men to ruin.

"A minute ago you had eggplant in paradise; now you're sending it to hell," commented one astute observer.

And the poet, an early prophet of mass media, set things straight: "I am the courtier of the sultan, not the courtier of the eggplant."

# Against the Current

The ideas in the weekly *Marcha* tended to be red; its balance sheet was a whole lot redder. Hugo Alfaro, besides being a journalist, sometimes filled in as manager and had the demoralizing task of paying the bills. Once in a great while Hugo would jump for joy: "We've got the issue covered!"

Advertisers had come through. In the world of independent journalism, a miracle of that order is celebrated as proof that God exists.

But the editor, Carlos Quijano, would blanch. Horror of horrors; there was no news as bad as that news. To run advertisements meant sacrificing a page or more, and he needed every sacred column inch to question certainties, yank off masks, stir up hornets' nests, and help make tomorrow more than just another name for today.

After thirty-four years in print, *Marcha* ceased to exist when the military dictatorship that overran Uruguay put an end to such lunacy.

# The Hatmaker

The telephone rang. I heard a gruff voice say, "I can't believe the mistake you made. Listen, I'm not kidding, mistakes happen and can happen to anyone, but not like that . . ."

My heart sank. I couldn't speak. My book on soccer had just come out, and in my country everyone has a Ph.D. on the subject. I closed my eyes and prepared for the worst.

"The 1930 World Cup," said the raspy, relentless voice.

"Yes," I mumbled.

"It was in July."

"Yes."

"And what's the weather like in Montevideo in July?"

"Cold."

"Very cold," the voice corrected. Then the attack: "And you wrote that the stadium was a sea of straw hats! Straw? Felt! They were felt!"

The voice calmed down, recollected: "I was there that afternoon. We won four-two, I can see it now. But that's not why I'm calling. I'm calling because I'm a hatmaker, have been all my life . . . and a lot of those hats were mine."

# The Hat

Whenever he wore his hat, Manuel Zequeira looked in the mirror and saw nothing but his hat.

The poet knew that it made him invisible. The rest of Havana disagreed, but the poet didn't think much of other people's opinions.

With his hat on, Manuel would barge into homes and bars, kiss forbidden lips and eat the food of others without the least concern for the furies he unleashed. And in July, when the city boiled, he would walk the streets wearing not a stitch besides the hat and pay no attention to the stones thrown at him. As long as they missed his hat, he felt nothing.

The hat, sauntering through the air, was the only part of him that would live on after he died.

# The Chosen Lady

He wasn't born within her, but for her he crossed the sea and lived his life in her streets.

People called him the Gentleman from Paris, though he was a Galician from Lugo.

He accepted no handouts. The sunshine with which she blessed him more than satisfied his hunger.

As a sign of his love, he vowed never to cut his hair or shave his beard, which reached down to his feet. And to show due obedience, he promised to move every once in a while. Carrying his belongings in a couple of old canvas bags, the gentleman shifted from a bench in Christo Park to the steps of Sagrado Corazón Church, or set up his castle in some hidden corner of Caballería Dock.

On that dock, his dock, one historic afternoon he publicly pardoned the guerrillas of the Sierra Maestra for copying his beard, and he finished by reciting a few verses dedicated to his queen and lady.

To serve her and her many charms, the gentleman appointed himself her king of kings and lord of lords. To defend her, he declared war against her covetous enemies. Standing before the lions of the Paseo del Prado, surrounded by his halberdiers and a few curious passersby, he vowed to fight to the death and called out his fleet of gunships and armies of the dawn, the day, the dusk, and the night.

Now he lies in the ground at San Francisco convent alongside bishops, archbishops, clerics, and conquistadores.

He was buried in the place of honor he deserved by Eusebio Leal, who was always crazy about her too.

The Gentleman rests within her now, the haughty bedraggled lady Havana, who watches over his sleep.

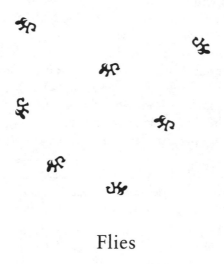

# Flies

José Miguel Corchado's body is chock-full of questions. Years ago he lost count of the relentless questions that pester him, but he remembers the day the first one worked its way inside him.

It happened in Seville on a sunny afternoon redolent, as you might imagine, with the fragrance of orange blossoms: an afternoon like all others, at the end of a working day like all other working days. He was alone, walking home through the crowd, immersed in a solitude like all other solitudes, when up popped the first question, buzzing like a fly. He tried to chase it away, but it kept circling around until it got under his skin and refused to come out. That night he couldn't sleep.

The following day, José Miguel sat in a chair and declared, "I'm not moving an inch until I know who I am."

# Exorcism

It happened in 1950. Against all predictions, against all indications, Brazil lost the World Cup on home turf, beaten by Uruguay.

After the final whistle, with darkness falling, the crowd remained seated in the stands of the brand-new Maracaná stadium. People sculpted in stone, a gigantic monument to defeat: the largest crowd ever in the history of soccer could not speak or move. The mourners stayed until late into the night.

Isaías Ambrosio was there. He was one of the workmen who had built the stadium and he'd been given a free ticket.

A half century later, Isaías is still there, tethered to the same spot in the empty grandstand.

Every day at the fatal hour, his lips pressed to an invisible microphone, broadcasting to an imaginary audience, Isaías recounts the play that brought defeat: every step, every painful detail. Then, in the tones of a radio commentator, he bellows out the fatal goal, the goooooooooooal, he wails it and wails it again, as he did the day before and will the day after and every day to follow.

# The Machine

Part radio, part telephone, and part clothes iron, complete with a wind-up handle and a microphone, Rúsvelt Nicodemo's machine was definitely high tech.

As Rúsvelt told it, the machine brought him back to life after his blood turned to jelly like blood sausage. From then on, he believed only in the machine.

Whenever he got permission to go out, Rúsvelt headed for Conde Street and would spend hours watching Santo Domingo's society girls go by.

There was one whose light always shone brighter than the rest, and he'd trail her glow, at a respectful distance.

One night the machine, which never lied, told him, "She adores you."

At the next corner Rúsvelt crossed to cut the girl off. "How long are you going to go on pretending you don't care? Your lips say nothing, but I hear the voice of your heart."

The machine confirmed, "She's dying for you."

But the moment she caught sight of him, she took off at top speed. Rúsvelt lost patience and ran after her shouting, "Coward, temptress, liar." Not from disappointment but from indignation. He could not stand playacting.

His outings always ended the same way. An awful beating and back to the asylum in Nigua.

The machine consoled him, "If women were necessary, God would have one."

# The Evil Eye

His tractor broke down: it had to happen sometime.

His crop failed: the weather didn't help.

But when the run of bad luck hit his cow and the calf was still-born, Antonio was certain: his neighbors had put the evil eye on him.

It couldn't just be a plain and simple evil eye. Too efficient. Antonio figured his enemies had cast the spell from some apparatus that looked like a television but wasn't one. He searched the town of Ambia for this electronic eye, studying the antennae house by house. He couldn't find it.

He had no alternative but to move to the forest, where there was no electricity.

He girded his fortress with holly and garlic cloves and bottles stuffed with bread and a huge necklace of salt, and he carpeted the inside with crosses of every size and portraits of Galicia's most famous soccer players.

And in the door he plunged the knife that cuts through envy.

# Looking at Miró

Almir D'Avila came in as a child, was declared insane, and never left.

No one ever wrote him a letter, no one ever paid him a visit.

Though he might like to leave, he has nowhere to go; though he might like to talk, he has no one to talk to.

For over forty years, he has spent his days in the São Paulo asylum walking in circles, a transistor radio pressed to his ear. Along the way he always meets the same men walking in circles, each with a transistor pressed to his ear.

One of the doctors organized a field trip to see Joan Miró's paintings.

Almir put on his only suit, threadbare but well ironed by his mattress, pulled his admiral's hat down over his eyes, and set off with the others.

And he saw. He saw exploding colors, a tomato with a mustache, a dancing fork, a bird that was a naked woman, the heavens with eyes, faces with stars.

He looked at painting after painting and frowned. It seemed Miró was a disappointment, and the doctor wanted to know why.

"Too much," said Almir.

"Too much what?"

"Too much craziness."

# Not Looking

For over a year, Titina Benavidez couldn't find the strength to lift her eyelids.

In the hospital they thought it could be ataxia, a rare condition, but tests ruled it out. The opthamologist found nothing.

Titina, eyes shut day and night, remained cloistered at her family's farm on the outskirts of Las Piedras.

Perhaps her eyes had lost the will to go on looking. Nobody knows. What we do know is that her healthy young heart lost the will to go on beating.

On December 31, 2000, Titina died, as the year, the century, and the millennium died, perhaps as tired as she of seeing what they saw.

# Seeing

On the open plains of Salto, the supervisor, now getting on in years, had a reputation for seeing what no one else could.

Carlos Santalla asked him, with all due respect, Sir, if it was true what people said, that he saw things that were invisible because he had a broad mind. So broad, people said, that it was too big for his skull and gave him headaches.

The elderly gaucho laughed loudly. "I'll tell you this, I'm curious and I'm lucky. The narrower my vision gets, the more I see."

Carlos was nine at the time. When he was about to turn one hundred, he still remembered it. For him, too, the years had narrowed his vision and he saw more.

## Points of View

Somewhere in time, beyond time, the world was gray. Thanks to the Ishir Indians, who stole color from the gods, the world today is resplendent with colors that dazzle the eyes of all who look at them.

Ticio Escobar lent a hand to a film crew that came to the Chaco to shoot scenes of daily life among the Ishir.

An Indian girl pursued the director, a silent shadow glued to his side, staring into his face as if she wanted to jump into his strange blue eyes.

The director turned to Ticio, who knew the girl and understood her language. Through him, she confessed, "I want to know what colors you see."

The director smiled. "The same as you."

"And how do you know what colors I see?"

# Colors

Gods and devils merge in the crowd, coming and going in the variegated flow of the many. Here nobody has a job but everybody has lots to do.

The light shouts, the air dances. Each person is a walking color. The black bodies cast green and blue shadows, and the glorious breeze contains so many shades that the rainbow hides its head for fear of looking foolish.

Above the sea, splashed across the slopes of the flayed mountains, Port-au-Prince presents itself to the eyes as a shrill palette of color, where life gets distracted and forgets how little it lasts and how much it hurts.

Could it be that the city imitates the artists who paint the city? Or is it without help of any kind that she transforms her garbage into beauty?

# A Dictionary of Colors

According to the surviving Indians on the banks of the Paraguay River, plumage provides color and power.

Green parrot feathers confer style on whoever wears them, and they revive dying plants.

If it weren't for the pink feathers of the spoonbill bird, the cactus would bear no pears.

Black duck feathers are good for softening bad moods.

White swan feathers chase away pests.

The macaw's red feathers call down the rain, and his yellow ones summon good news.

And the sad gray feathers of the rhea give verve to the human song.

# The Sevencolors

Dante D'Ottone was walking through Rodó Park, wandering among the trees, when he spied a woman kneeling before an enormous telescope pointed at the lake.

"Excuse me . . . may I?"

The woman pulled away from the lens. "Take a look."

And Dante discovered the sevencolors, a little bird you never see in Montevideo, fluttering over the lake.

She told him she'd wanted a pair of binoculars because she liked bird-watching so much, but she couldn't afford them. One Sunday at the Tristán Narvaja flea market she found this telescope amid a lot of other old junk, and for a few pesos it was hers.

The sevencolors flitted about unawares, while the telescope pursued that jubilance of the air.

# The King

In a park in Gijón, someone calls from the treetops.

When all but the whispering breeze in the leaves has receded, a cry that sounds human breaks the silence.

It is the night call of the peacock.

During the day, he flaunts his splendors. Dragging his long feathered tail, always dressed for a party, the cock struts and preens. When he spins around and fans his leafy blue-green crown of a tail, his luminous beauty thrills passersby and humbles every other bird in the park.

Ducks, drakes, swans, geese, pigeons, and sparrows all move as a flock flying or swimming on the lake. Together they chat, eat, sleep. But the peacock lives alone, far from other peacocks, and he seeks out no one.

He who was born to be looked at looks at no one.

When night falls and the people have gone, he flies to the highest branch of an empty tree, and he sleeps. Alone.

Then he calls out.

# Art History

"Look, Papa! Oxen!"

Marcelino Sautuola craned his neck. In the light from his lantern, he made them out. Oxen they weren't. On the roof of the cave, painted by deft hands, were bison, elk, horses, and wild boars.

Not long after, Sautuola published a pamphlet on the paintings he'd discovered, thanks to his daughter, in a cave at Altamira. They were, he claimed, prehistoric art.

From all corners came speleologists, archaeologists, paleontologists, anthropologists; no one believed him. They said the paintings were done by an artist friend of Sautuola's or some other practical joker from the European art scene.

Later on, it all became clear. The Paleolithic hunters of long ago pursued more than their prey. As a spell to ward off hunger and fear, or just because, they also pursued beauty in flight.

# Memory in Stone

In the depths of a cave by the Pinturas River, a hunter pressed his bloodstained hand to the stone wall. The handprint marked a moment of truce between the urgency of killing and the terror of dying. Sometime later, next to that print, another hunter laid his soot-blackened hand. And other hunters followed, leaving the stone wall dotted with prints the color of blood, ashes, earth, or plants.

Thirteen thousand years later, near the Pinturas River in the town of Perito Moreno, someone writes on a wall, "I was here."

# The Painter

Güiscardo Améndola, a fellow from the neighborhood, was going to paint a mural in a bar on the waterfront. He invited me to come along.

He didn't bring a box of paints or brushes or a ladder or anything. This wasn't how I imagined Michelangelo on his way to the Sistine Chapel, but my youth gave me no right to ask questions.

A large black wall awaited us.

Améndola climbed up on a chair and from his pocket pulled out a coin with a serrated edge. Coin in hand, he went on the attack. The sharp edge scored the wall with long white lines that crisscrossed without rhyme or reason. Clueless, I watched him thrust and parry. After a few more lunges, I saw a lighthouse appear out of the blackness, a powerful lighthouse rising above the rocks to illuminate the waves.

That lighthouse, born from a coin, would go on to save many a sailor from shipwreck, be they on deck or leaning drunkenly against the bar.

# The Photographer

He was a soccer player for Cuba's national team when a ball to the head knocked him flat.

He looked to be dead. Sometime later he woke up in the hospital. Alive. Blind.

Now Hiladio Sánchez is a photographer. Camera in hand, he turns his magical touch to visual imagery. He chooses the subject that sounds best, paces off the distance, and adjusts the shutter according to the heat of the sun. And when everything is ready, he shoots.

Hiladio photographs the sunlight that governs hours and people as they pass.

He does not photograph moonlight. Every night, those freezing fingers touch his face. And the blind man plays deaf.

# The Sculptors

Piltriquitrón Hill has its head in the clouds. Until recently charred ruins, that head is now a forest of carvings.

After one of the blazing fires that are now so common in Patagonia, sculptors came from all around, climbed the peak, and set to work on the fallen, dismembered trunks.

Were the trees dead, or just playing dead? For a week, day in day out, the sculptors kept at their task, until the grace and magic of their hands turned the cemetery into theater.

The show begins with a welcome from a gigantic trunk that's now a jester sprawled flat, wearing a single hat on its two heads. Visitors roam from tree to tree, past the wooden bodies that from the ruins rise, and in the ruins play.

# Kites

The rainy season is ending, the weather cooling off, the corn ripe and ready in the fields. And the kite artists of the town of Santiago Sacatepéquez are giving their creations a final touch.

The largest, prettiest kites in the world are the work of many hands, and each is unique.

When the Day of the Dead dawns, these immense birds of paper plumage take flight and soar, until they break free of the strings that hold them and vanish into the heavens.

On the ground, at every graveside, people tell their dead relatives the latest gossip. The dead don't answer. They're busy enjoying the spectacle on high, where kites in the sky have the good fortune of becoming wind.

# The Price of Art

Europe was kind enough to civilize black Africa. First, it smashed the map and swallowed the pieces, stole the gold, the ivory, the diamonds, kidnapped Africa's strongest children and then sold them into slavery.

Then, to complete their education, Europe treated black Africans to numerous punitive military expeditions.

At the end of the nineteenth century, British soldiers carried out one such pedagogical incursion in the kingdom of Benin. After the butchery and before the burning, they carted off the booty: a phenomenal quantity of masks, sculptures, and carvings, torn from the sanctuaries that gave them life and shelter.

It was the largest body of African art ever collected, covering a thousand years of history. In London, the disturbing beauty of these works evoked some curiosity and nothing in the way of admiration. The output of the African zoo was of interest to only a few eccentric collectors and museums specializing in primitive customs. Nevertheless, when Queen Victoria auctioned the treasures off, the take was enough to pay for the entire military expedition.

Thus the art of Benin financed the devastation of the kingdom where it had been born and bred.

# First Music

It sounded like mosquitoes in summer, but it wasn't summer.

One night in 1964 Arno Penzias and Robert Wilson could not work in peace. On top of a ridge in the Appalachians the two astronomers were trying to capture radio waves emitted by who knows which impossibly far-off galaxy, but the buzz from their antenna made their ears hurt.

Later on they figured it out. The buzz was the echo of the explosion that gave birth to the universe. What made the antenna vibrate weren't mosquitoes, but the very blast that began time and space and the planets and everything else. And who knows, but I'd venture to say that the echo still resounded in the air because it wanted us to hear it, since we little Earth people are also echoes of that long-ago cry of the newborn universe.

# The Price of Progress

Apollo, sun of the Greeks, was the god of music.

He invented the lyre, which put flutes to shame. When he plucked its strings, he conveyed to mortals the secrets of life and death.

One day his most musical son discovered that strings of ox gut sound better than those of linen.

Alone with his lyre, Apollo tried them out. He strummed the new strings and confirmed their superiority.

Then the god treated his palate to nectar and ambrosia, picked up his war bow, took aim at his son from afar, and split the boy's chest in half.

# Flutes

Dance life away, eat life away; the city of Sibari in the south of what we now call Italy was once devoted to music and good food.

But the Sibaris wanted to be warriors. They dreamed of conquest, and Sibari ended up destroyed. Crotone, the enemy city, erased it from the map twenty-five centuries ago.

On the shores of the Gulf of Taranto the final battle was fought.

The Sibaris, trained in music, were by music defeated.

When the Sibari cavalry charged, the Crotone soldiers unsheathed their flutes. The galloping horses recognized the melody. They stopped short, reared up, and began to dance. It wasn't the most opportune moment, given the circumstances, but the horses kept on dancing, as was their custom and pleasure, while the horsemen fled and the flutes went on trilling.

# The Dance

Helena was dancing inside a music box where hoop-skirted ladies and bewigged gentlemen twirled and bowed and spun. The porcelain figurines were a bit ridiculous, but they were pretty and it was fun to pirouette with them in time to the whirling music, until Helena tripped and fell and broke.

The blow woke her up. Her left foot hurt like hell. She tried to get up and couldn't walk. Her ankle was swollen and sore.

"I fell down in another country," she confessed, "and in another time."

But she didn't say that to the doctor.

# Drummings

Like dreams, drums resound in the night.

In the Americas, slave revolts were hatched by day, to the beat of the lash, and they exploded at night, to the beat of the drum.

When the French burned alive a rebel named Makandal, who had stirred up the blacks of Haiti, it was drums that announced he had turned himself into a mosquito and escaped the blaze.

The masters did not understand the language of drumbeats, but all too well they knew how demonic rhythms passed on forbidden news and summoned secret gods or even the Devil himself, who danced to the beat with bells on his ankles.

The masters never did learn that on the full moon the drum played itself, with no hands. In those moments, when the drum beat the drum, the dead arose to listen to the wonder.

# The Piano

When the city of Tarija was populated by fourteen thousand nine hundred and fifty servants and fifty for them to serve, the only woman being served who didn't own a piano was Doña Beatriz Arce de Baldiviezo.

A concerned uncle sent her a Steinway from Paris, to help her regain her color and composure, for she was green with envy and consumed by sighs.

Packed in one immense box, the piano traveled by ship, by train, and then by shoulder. It was hand-carried deep into Bolivia: forty peons bushwhacked across the sierra saddled with the weight, improvising bridges, stairs, and paths. For five months they made the atrocious trek through gorges and up and down ravines, until the gift arrived at last, without a scratch, at the home of Doña Beatriz.

It wasn't just any old piano. The Steinway had been baptized by the hands of Franz Liszt, and was adorned with awards won in several European kingdoms.

Years passed; people passed. With time, Tarija grew and changed.

And one day María Nidi Baldiviezo, who had inherited the piano, left her doctor's office diagnosed with cancer.

Of the family fortune, only the piano and nostalgia remained, so Doña María put the piano up for sale to pay for her trip to the hospital in Houston.

The first bid came from Japan. She turned it down. The second came from the United States, and she refused it. The third prospective buyer called from Germany, and she wouldn't budge. It was the same with offers from Buenos Aires, La Paz, and Santa Cruz. The seller said no to the low bids, no to the high bids, and no to those in the middle.

From her sickbed, Doña María called together Tarija's music lovers, theater lovers, art lovers, and other lovers and made them a proposition: "Give me whatever you have, and the Steinway is yours."

Doña María died with neither trip nor treatment.

The piano had no desire to leave Tarija. There it found love, and there it remains, giving service at cultural events, patriotic ceremonies, and all the city's public occasions.

# The Harmonium

To get to Buenos Aires, Hermógenes Cayo walked thousands of miles from the distant heights of Juyjuy. He made the trip in 1946 together with other Indians fighting for their land; on impulse he stopped at Luján, where he'd heard there was a cathedral that would knock you over.

When he got home, he erected a Luján cathedral in miniature at the entrance to his stone house. He made the Gothic arches out of adobe and the stained-glass windows from bits of broken bottles, using all the colors he could find. The copy turned out identical to the original, only a bit better. Jorge Pelorán took pictures to prove it.

Years later, Hermógenes heard a harmonium in a church somewhere.

Never in his life had he heard a harmonium, and now he discovered that he could not live without one.

But the people are few and the miles many up there on the high plain, and the church with the harmonium was several days' walk away. So Hermógenes convinced the priest that his instrument was out of tune, and claiming to be an expert, he offered his services to put it right. He took the harmonium apart, carefully sketched each piece, and back home built his own instrument, carved entirely out of wood from the giant cactus.

Every afternoon from then on, his harmonium bid the day farewell.

# The Electrician

He traveled the paths of the pampa by bicycle, with a ladder on his back. Bautista Riolfo was an electrician and a handyman, a Mister Fix-It who repaired tractors, watches, grinding mills, radios, rifles. The hump on his back came from stooping over sockets, gearboxes, and other rarities.

René Favorolo, the only doctor around, was also a handyman. With the few instruments in his satchel and the medicines at hand he filled the role of cardiologist, surgeon, midwife, psychiatrist, and all-round specialist in whatever needed fixing.

One fine day, René went to Bahía Blanca and brought home an instrument never before seen in those solitudes inhabited only by the wind and the dust.

The record player had its quirks. After a couple of months it stopped working.

Along came Bautista on his bicycle. He sat on the ground, scratched his chin, poked around, soldered a few wires, tightened a few screws and nuts. "Now give it a try," he said.

René chose a recording of Beethoven's Ninth and placed the needle on his favorite part.

Music filled the house, spilling through the open window into the deserted night, and it lived on in the air after the record stopped spinning.

René said something or asked something, but Bautista didn't answer.

Bautista had his face buried in his hands.

A long moment passed before the electrician was able to say, "Pardon me, Don René, but I never heard anything like that. I didn't know there was such . . . such electricity in this world."

# The Singer

When Alfredo Zitarrosa died in Montevideo, his friend Juceca accompanied him to the gates of Paradise so he wouldn't have to face the proceedings alone. When he came back, Juceca told us what he'd heard.

Saint Peter asked for his name, age, and occupation.

"Singer," said Alfredo.

Singer of what, the gatekeeper wanted to know.

"Milongas," said Alfredo.

Saint Peter hadn't heard of them. His curiosity was pricked, though. "Sing," he ordered.

Alfredo sang a milonga, then another, then a hundred. Saint Peter didn't want him to stop. Having for so long strummed the earth, Alfredo's voice now strummed the heavens.

God, who was out somewhere shepherding clouds, cupped his ear. Juceca said it was the only time God wasn't sure who God was.

# The Songstress

Liliana Villagra had been trying for a long while to fall asleep, wanting to but unable, and after a lot of tossing and turning and fighting with her pillow she heard the clock strike three and needed air. She got up, opened the window wide.

All the snow of all the winters that ever there were had fallen on Paris. Pigalle was always a noisy neighborhood, ringing with quarrels and carousing, the comings and goings of whores and transvestites. But that night Pigalle was a white desert, inscribed with the pattern of passing steps.

Then a song rose up from the snow to the window: a voice like a little bird's crooning a sad old melody. It was a woman leaning against the wall, waiting for customers. A few snowflakes drifted down on rue Houdon and landed on the flea-market leather coat she held open, baring her body to the empty street.

Leaning out the window, Liliana offered her coffee: "Would you like to come in?"

"Thanks, but I can't. I'm working."

"Nice song," said Liliana.

"I sing to keep from falling asleep."

# The Song

Prague was mute.

On the corner where Celetnà Street gives onto the great plaza of the Old City, a voice suddenly split open the hush of the night.

From a wheelchair moored amid the cobblestones, a woman was singing.

I had never heard such a voice, so beautiful and so strange, a voice from another world, and I pinched myself. Was I dreaming? What world was I in?

I got my answer from a group of young men who came up behind me. They taunted the crippled singer, mimicking her and laughing themselves silly. She fell silent.

# Another Song

Ren Weschler took down his story. In 1975 Breyten Breyten-
bach was the only white prisoner among the many blacks on death
row in the Pretoria jail.

At the end of each night, one of the condemned would be
marched to the gallows. Before the floor opened beneath his feet,
the man would sing. Every dawn, Breyten awoke to a different
song. Alone in his cell, he listened to the voice of the man about to
die.

Breyten lived. He hears it still.

# Mermaids

Don Julián lived alone on the loneliest of the islands of Xochimilco, in a thatch hut watched over by dolls and dogs.

The dolls, picked up in garbage dumps, hung legless or armless from the trees. They protected him from evil spirits. The four skinny dogs defended him from evil people. But neither dolls nor dogs knew how to scare off the mermaids.

From the depths of the waters they called to him.

Don Julián knew a few spells. Whenever the mermaids came to carry him off, chanting his name over and over, he chased them away by singing back:

*I'm telling you, I'm telling you,*
*the Devil can take me, God can too,*
*but never you, no never you.*

And also:

*Back to the brine, back to the brine,*
*give other lips your fatal kiss,*
*but never mine, no never mine.*

One afternoon after plowing the earth to plant squash, Don Julián went to the water's edge to fish. He caught a huge one, a fish he knew because twice before it had got away. Taking out the hook, he heard voices he also knew.

"Julián, Julián, Julián," they sang, as always. And as always, Julián leaned out over the water above the shimmering pink intruders, and he opened his mouth to intone his unfailing response.

But nothing came out. This time, nothing came out.

Deserted by the music, his body was seen drifting among the islands.

# Ballads

In the days when it took a horse to carry a tape recorder, Lauro Ayestarán crisscrossed the countryside collecting musical memories.

In search of lost ballads, Lauro once went to a hut hidden in the far-off realms of Tacuarembó. There lived a gaucho who had been a dancer and guitar player, and a champion dueler in verse.

The man was ancient. He no longer went from town to town and fair to fair. He walked little and fell down a lot, and to get up he had to lean on the back of one of his dogs. He couldn't see. Neither could he sing; he sort of mouthed the words. But he was known as one who remembers.

"Up here there's nothing missing," he whispered, tapping his head with his finger.

Guitar in hand, barely brushing the strings, the old man recited, purred, hummed. In the late afternoon, a dry rasp celebrated the memory of free men and cattle on the range.

Round and round went the wheels of the tape recorder. The blind balladeer listened to the whirr without comment, until at last he asked what was buzzing.

"It's a machine that keeps voices alive," explained Ayestarán. He rewound the tape, and the verses rang out again.

For the first time in his life, the old man heard his own voice.

He didn't like the imitation one bit.

# The Idol

Some nights in the cafés, the competition was fierce.

"Me, when I was a child, I got peed on by a lion," one said in a low voice, making light of his tragedy.

"Me, what I liked best was walking on walls," said another, complaining that at home this pastime was forbidden.

And another: "Me, as a kid I wrote love poems. Then I lost them on a train. And who do you think found them? Neruda."

Don Arnaldo, an orthodontist, refused to be cowed. Elbows on the bar, he let slip a name: "Libertad Lamarque."

He paused for impact, then, "Sound familiar?"

And he recalled his meeting with the woman known as Latin America's Sweetheart.

Don Arnaldo wasn't lying. One morning back in the thirties, the singer and actress was taking an awful beating in a hotel in Santiago, Chile. Her husband was slapping her across the face, just to keep her in line, and in between two punches Libertad screamed, "Enough! It's your doing!" and dove out the fourth-floor window. She bounced off an awning and landed on top of the orthodontist, who was walking on the sidewalk below, on his way home from visiting his mother. Libertad landed in one piece, along with her damask robe embroidered with Chinese dragons. But Don Arnaldo, crushed, was taken by ambulance to the hospital.

Once his broken bones had healed and his mummy's bandages came off, Don Arnaldo began telling the story that he went on telling until the end of his days, in cafés and anywhere else he could find an ear. The shooting star had thrown herself, from the heavens above, from the high clouds where the goddesses of ether and footlights dwell, down to Earth, and of the millions of men walking the planet she had chosen him. Yes, him. And had collapsed in his arms, so she wouldn't die alone.

# The Movies

Geraldine was working on a film in a village in the mountains of Turkey.

The first afternoon she went out for a walk. Practically no one was about. A few men, no women at all. Then, turning a corner, she found herself face-to-face with a gang of teenagers.

Geraldine looked left, looked right, looked behind her. She was surrounded, no escape. Her throat refused to scream. Speechless, she offered what she had: watch, money.

The boys laughed. No, that wasn't what they wanted. And speaking something more or less like English, they asked if she was really Chaplin's daughter.

Astonished, she nodded. Only then did she notice that they all had little charcoal mustaches, and that the sticks they carried were meant to be canes.

The show began.

And they were all him.

# Movie Buffs

There was a crowd of people at the entrance to Havana's Yara cinema, and a policeman was trying to get them to form a line. His intentions were laudable, even heroic, but not very realistic. Every time he managed to get them lined up, they would spill out once again.

The officer was on his own, impotent against their passion for the movies and for chaos. Then his commanding voice made itself heard: "Back!" the policeman barked. "Ladies and gentlemen, the line begins behind the wall!"

"What wall?" people asked, bewildered.

The guardian of order explained, "If there's no wall . . . just imagine one."

# Television

At the end of 1999, the president of Uruguay cut the ribbon at a brand-new school in Pinar Norte.

Since it was a neighborhood of the working poor, the country's chief executive came to add some luster to the ceremony.

The president appeared from the heavens, by helicopter, accompanied by a TV crew.

In his speech he paid homage to the children of the fatherland, our most valuable asset, and he underscored the importance of education, the most profitable investment we can make in such a competitive world. After that everyone sang the national anthem and released a raft of colored balloons.

Then came the climax, when the president presented each student with a toy.

This was all broadcast live.

When the cameras stopped rolling, the president ascended back to the heavens. And the school officials proceeded to collect the toys he'd given out. It was not easy to pry them from the children's hands.

# The Theater

Aristophanes wandered all over Chiapas, chatting with the locals. Anton Chekhov trekked through the desert of San Luis Potosí, his characters in tow.

They had never been to such places before.

It was the actors of El Galpón who took them from one end of Mexico to the other.

The entire El Galpón company was there in exile. Those were years of filth and fear under Uruguay's military dictatorship, and when the troupe left Montevideo, they took along everything but their theater.

The theater, which they'd built themselves without a cent of help from the government, stayed behind, but El Galpón did not and neither did the audience. The generals put on their shows for the empty seats. Shadow without a body: body without a soul; no one went.

# The Theatergoer

Gonzalo Muñoz, whose sepia photo is in my family album, was born to live by night and sleep by day.

His nights were spent wide-eyed, keeping the ghosts company, but during the day he always had a lot to do, so he had to settle for catnaps. He'd drop off at any moment, and upon waking he wouldn't know the time of day or even what sort of being he was. Sometimes, Don Gonzalo, who lived like an owl, crowed from the roof in the middle of the afternoon, like a rooster greeting the dawn. This did not go down well with the neighbors.

One evening he attended the opening of a play at Montevideo's Solís Theater. It was a formal affair with a company from Europe. During the second act he fell asleep. He nodded off just when the main character, a foul-tempered husband, crouched behind a screen, pistol in hand. A short while later, when the unfaithful wife came onstage, the husband sprang from his hiding place and fired. The bullets brought down the sinner and woke up Don Gonzalo, who stood in the middle of the audience, threw his arms wide, and exclaimed: "Hold it right there! Don't anybody move! Ladies and gentlemen, don't be afraid, please stay where you are!"

His wife, seated at his side, sank into the depths of her chair.

# The Actor

Horacio Tubio built his house in a valley called El Bolsón.

The house had no electricity. Horacio had come from California with all his modern gadgets, but the computer, fax, television, and washing machine refused to work by candle power.

Horacio found the right office. An engineer received him. The man consulted several unfathomable maps and informed Horacio that electric service was already up and running in that area.

"Sure, it's up and running," Horacio allowed. "It's all over the forest. The trees are happy as clams."

The engineer took offense and fumed, "You know what your problem is? You're arrogant. Talking like that you're never going to get anywhere."

And he showed Horacio the way out.

Horacio backed away, shut the door behind him.

A moment later the engineer heard a knock.

It was Horacio, on his knees, his head bowed. "Mr. Engineer, you who have had the good fortune to have studied . . ."

"Get up, get up."

"You who have a degree . . ."

"Get up, please."

"Have pity, Mr. Engineer. I wish I too could learn to read . . ."

Horacio kept it up until his house got electricity.

# The Actress

More than half a century ago, the National Theater took *Blood Wedding* to the countryside of Salto.

The play, by Federico García Lorca, came from another countryside, the distant hinterland of Andalusia. It is a tragedy about feuding families: a broken engagement, a stolen bride, a jealous stabbing over a woman. The mother of one of the dead men turns to her neighbor: "Will you shut up? I want no wailing in this house. Your tears are nothing but water from your eyes."

Margarita Xirgu played the proud, pained mother onstage.

When the applause subsided, a hired hand from a large ranch approached Margarita, head bowed, hat in hand, and told her, "I understand how you feel. I also lost a son."

# That Applause

After García Lorca was riddled with bullets at the dawn of the Spanish Civil War, *The Shoemaker's Prodigious Wife* was never produced in his country. Many years later a Uruguayan troupe took the show to Madrid.

They acted with all their heart and soul.

At the curtain, there was no applause. Instead, the audience began to stamp their feet wildly. The actors did not understand.

One of them, China Zorrilla, told the story: "We were shocked. A disaster. It was enough to make you cry."

Then the ovation began, long, grateful. Still the actors didn't understand.

Maybe that thundering of feet on the ground was applause for the playwright. For the playwright executed for being a pinko, a fag, a weirdo. Maybe it was a way of saying, "Listen, Federico. Hear how alive you are."

# The Comedy of the Half Millennium

PERFORMANCE TODAY! DON'T MISS IT!: Portugal went all out to celebrate the five hundredth anniversary of the arrival of Bartolomeu Dias on the southern coast of Africa. The country became a vast theater of imperial nostalgia, and center stage was the intrepid navigator who reached the Cape of Good Hope in 1487, a time of supreme glory, when God bestowed on Portugal half the world.

Actors, dressed in period costumes of silks and velvets with fine swords and many-feathered caps, filled an exact replica of the ship in which Bartolomeu Dias put to sea and set sail for Africa.

On a South African beach, according to the script, a crowd of blacks was to jump for grateful joy for the explorers who five centuries earlier had done them the favor of discovering them. But in 1987 the beach was reserved for whites only. Under apartheid, blacks were not allowed.

A euphoric throng of whites, painted black, welcomed the Portuguese.

# The Comedy of the Century

In 1889 Paris celebrated the hundredth anniversary of the French Revolution with a grand world's fair.

Argentina sent a varied display of the country's products. Among them was a family of Indians from Tierra del Fuego. They were eleven Ona Indians, rare examples of an endangered species: at that moment the last Onas were being hunted down with Winchester rifles.

Of the eleven, two died en route. The survivors were exhibited in an iron cage. "South American Anthropophagi," the sign read. For the first few days they were given nothing to eat. The Indians howled with hunger. Then they were tossed bits of raw meat. It was beef, but it made for a horrifying spectacle. The onlookers, who had paid to get in, crowded around the cage to watch the savage cannibals wrestle over the food.

Thus was celebrated the first hundred years of the Declaration of the Rights of Man.

# The Comedy of the Half Century

It was the fiftieth anniversary of the atomic explosions that annihilated Hiroshima and Nagasaki.

The Smithsonian Institution in Washington announced plans for a large exhibit.

The display would include documentary information and comments from scientists, historians, and military experts. It would feature statements by the protagonists, from the colonel who commanded the bombers and lost no sleep over the affair, to several Japanese survivors, who lost sleep and everything else.

Visitors to the exhibit would run the risk of learning that the masses murdered from the sky were mostly women and children. Worse yet, the background information might lead them to conclude that the bombs were dropped not to win the war, because the war was already won, but to intimidate the Soviet Union, soon to become the next enemy.

To avoid such grave dangers, the show was announced but never mounted. Everything was dropped but an exhibition of the *Enola Gay,* the plane that dropped the bomb on Hiroshima, so that fervent patriots could kiss it on the nose.

# The Tailor

He swore he would fly. He swore on all the buttonholes he'd ever opened and all the buttons he'd ever placed and all the suits and dresses and coats he'd ever measured, cut, basted, and sewn, stitch by stitch, day after day his entire life.

From then on, Reichelt the tailor spent his time sewing a pair of enormous bat wings. The wings folded so they'd fit in the grotty hole where he worked and lived.

At long last, after a huge effort, the elaborate cloth-covered framework of pipes and metal rods was ready.

The tailor spent the night unable to sleep, praying to God to give him a windy day. And in the morning, a gusty morning in the year 1912, he climbed to the tip of the Eiffel Tower, spread his wings, and flew to his death.

# The Airplane

Flags fluttered high in the breeze.

Officials chased off the cows grazing on the runway.

No one was missing. The entire town of Lorica had been waiting for hours. In lace, bows, neckties, everybody was starched as if for a wedding or a baptism, their eyes glued to the sky, all roasting in the sun without a word of complaint.

From afar, they saw it coming. And they swallowed hard. And when the one they were waiting for touched down, the battle roar and the whiplash of wind caused a stampede.

No airplane had ever come to Lorica.

The throng, mouths open, peered into the cloud of red dust and made out something shiny. The propellers came to a stop. A brave spectator broke ranks, ran toward the thing never before seen, and reported back that it smelled of soap.

When the bands struck up, two at once, the first playing the national anthem, the second a medley of vallenatos, people rushed forward. They carried off the passengers on their shoulders and drowned the pilot in a sea of flowers. In celebration of the apparition come from the heavens, they started pouring drinks, whooping it up, and the party was on.

The airplane had landed for a short stopover on its way to other destinations, but it couldn't take off.

"That was the first hijacking in the history of Colombia," says David Sánchez-Juliao, the youngest of the hijackers.

# Flight Without a Map

She was an airplane. On her back, lying flat, she flew.

Suddenly she realized she'd lost her way, and couldn't even re-call where she was supposed to be going.

The passengers inside couldn't have cared less. They were all busy drinking, eating, smoking, talking, and dancing, because in her body there was plenty of room, the music was terrific, and nothing was out of bounds.

She wasn't worried either. She'd forgotten her destination, but the wings, her outstretched arms, grazed the moon as she whirled around the stars, turning circles in the heavens, and it was great fun to speed through the night to nowhere.

Helena woke up in bed, in the airport.

# Flight Plan

The doctor, Oriol Vall, was leaving. He'd spent a long while in Ajoya, deep in the mountains, taking part in village work and life, and the time had come to say farewell.

He went house by house. In the tiny dispensary, he stopped to explain things to María del Carmen, who had given him so much help.

"I'm going back to Spain, Doña María."

"Is Spain far away?"

She had never gone beyond the Gavilanes River. Oriol sketched a map to give her an idea. You have to cross the ocean, all the way across.

"It must be a very big boat for so much water."

He tried to explain with words and gestures. And María del Carmen, who had never seen an airplane, even from a distance, interrupted him: "Okay, I get it. What you mean is you're going to travel sleeping in the wind."

# The Train

"It's really strong," the father declared. "Like two hundred oxen."

The son, Simón de la Pava, saw a huge ribbon of smoke rising on the horizon.

Soon the powerful beast appeared. As she approached, she grew larger. She roared. She howled.

The child was terrified and tried to run away, but his father held him fast by the hand.

A squeal of metal on metal, a long moan, and the train came to a halt.

Simón and his father traveled from the valley of Ibagué to the high plain of Bogotá, from hot to cool and from cool to cold.

The journey lasted forever.

Snorting, the train drank rivers of water at every station. Then, wailing, sweating steam from her belly, she went back to lurching her way uphill.

The passengers reached their destination exhausted and covered in soot and dust.

While the father collected their suitcases, Simón approached the locomotive.

She was panting. He gave her a few pats on her hot rump, just to say thank you.

# The Passengers

Across fields and through the ages, the train rolled from Seville toward Morón de la Frontera. And from the window, the poet Julio Vélez observed with tired eyes the groves and houses that rushed by in bursts, while his memory wandered across geography and through time.

Seated across from Julio was a tourist. The tourist wanted to practice his stumbling Spanish, but Julio was off who knows where, searching for something or someone, a word or a woman he'd lost.

"Are you Andalusian?" the tourist asked.

Julio, absent, nodded.

And the tourist, intrigued, asked, "But if you're Andalusian, how come you're sad?"

# Are You There?

Two trains crashed into each other just outside London's Paddington Station.

A fireman fought his way on board with an ax and stepped into a car tipped on its side. Through the smoke, which added fog to the fog, he could see passengers strewn about like mannequins smashed to pieces amid the splintered wood and twisted steel. His flashlight moved across the debris searching in vain for some sign of life.

Not a moan could be heard. Nothing broke the silence except the ringing of cell phones, calling and calling and calling, from the pockets of the dead.

# Traffic Accident

Until well into the twentieth century, camels took care of transporting people and things on the island of Lanzarote.

The station, the Camel's Abode, was downtown in the port of Arrecife. As a child, Leandro Perdomo always walked past it on his way to school. He saw lots of camels lying or standing. One morning he counted forty, but he was never very good at math.

Back in those days, the island floated outside time, a world before the world, when people had time to waste time.

The camels came and went, plodding slowly through the immense black lava desert. They kept no schedule, had no fixed departure or arrival, but depart and arrive they did. And there were never any accidents. Never, that is, until one camel suffered a sudden attack of nerves and sent its passenger flying. The unfortunate woman split her head on a rock.

The camel had cracked because a strange thing had crossed its path, a beast that coughed, gave off smoke, and walked without legs.

It was the island's first automobile.

# Red, Yellow, Green

It happened overnight. Several poles, each with three eyes, sprouted up in the corners of the main street. The town of Quaraí had never seen anything like it before, nor had anywhere else in that region near the border.

The curious came on horseback. They tied up their horses on the outskirts, so as not to disrupt the traffic, and they sat down to view the novelty. Maté gourd in hand, thermos under arm, they waited for nightfall when lights are really lights and it is a pleasure to sit and watch, the way people sit and watch the stars come out in the sky. The lights turned on and off at the same steady pace, always the same three colors, one after the other. But those country men, indifferent to the passing cars and people, didn't weary of the spectacle.

"The one on that corner is prettier," someone suggested.

"This one here takes longer," offered another.

As far as we know, none of them asked what the lights were for, those magic eyes that blinked and blinked and blinked and never grew tired.

# Advertising

When Wagner Adoum drove his car, he always kept his eyes on the road ahead, without so much as a glance at the billboards yelling orders from the edges of Quito's streets and highways.

"I never killed anyone," he said. "And if I've reached the age I have, it's because I pay no attention to those billboards."

Thanks to his restraint, he explained, he managed to avoid dying from drowning, indigestion, hemorrhage, or suffocation. He didn't drink an ocean of Coca-Cola, or eat a mountain of hamburgers. Nor did he dig a crater in his belly by swallowing a million aspirins. And he kept credit cards from sinking him up to his ears in a swamp of debt.

# The Street

How many millions can squeeze onto a single street?

One day at noon, every person in Buenos Aires strode down Florida, the only walkable street left in the city. A drove of urbanoids had escaped from their jars, a multitude of legs zipping along, as if the refuge from the reign of motorcars would not last long.

In the middle of the crowd, Rogelio García Lupo noticed a man elbowing his way toward him with some difficulty. The man, a respectable-looking sort, threw his arms wide open. Rogelio, before he had a chance to think, was being hugged and hugging back. The man's face looked vaguely familiar. Rogelio could only manage to ask, "Who are we?"

# Map of the World

I was trying to decipher the racket of birdcalls in the trees at Stanford University when an elderly professor approached. The professor, learned in some scientific specialty, had a lot to say bottled up inside. In his field, he knew everything while I knew nothing, but he was friendly, spoke softly, and it was a pleasure to listen to him.

At some point, his curiosity got the better of him, and he asked me what country I was from. I answered, and from his startled eyes I could tell the name Uruguay was not too familiar. I was used to that, and the professor made some polite comment about the traditional dress in my country. It was obvious he was confusing Uruguay with Guatemala, which by some miracle was in the headlines at the time. I returned the favor by becoming Guatemalan on the spot, and without poking fun I said something or other about the tumultuous history of Central America.

"Central America," he said.

I wanted to believe he understood. Just in case, I didn't ask.

How well I know that many of his compatriots believe that Central America is Kansas City.

# Distances

Rafael Gallo, lord of the rings, had just finished a tough fight in the plaza at Albacete, where he won the ears and tail as trophies.

While taking off his suit of lights, the bullfighter declared, "We're going back to Seville right now."

His assistant explained they couldn't, it was too late. "Seville is so far away . . ."

Rafael leaped up, shaking his cape in his fist. "Ho-o-old it right there!"

Like a bolt of angry lightning, he set things straight. "Seville is just where it ought to be. It's this place that's far away."

# Geography

In Chicago, everybody's black. In New York, the midwinter sun bakes stones till they melt. In Brooklyn, anyone who reaches the age of thirty deserves a statue. The finest homes in Miami are built of trash. Hollywood is run by the rats.

Chicago, New York, Brooklyn, Miami, and Hollywood—these are the names of some of the barrios of Cité Soleil, the most abject slum in the capital of Haiti.

# The Geographer

"Lake Titicaca, you've heard of it?"

"I have."

"Lake Titicaca used to be here."

"Where?"

"Right here."

And he waved his arm at the endless parched terrain.

We were in the Tamarugal Desert, a landscape of bone-dry gravel extending from horizon to horizon, interrupted only once in a great while by the passing of a lizard. But who was I to contradict an expert?

My scientific curiosity was aroused. And the fellow was kind enough to explain how the lake had come to move so far away.

"I'm not sure when it happened. Before I was born. The herons took it."

One long raw winter, the lake froze without warning, and the herons' legs got stuck in the ice. After flapping their wings as hard as they could for many days and nights, the trapped birds finally managed to take off, but the lake went with them. Across the skies they flew carrying the frozen lake. When it melted, it fell to earth. And that's how it ended up way over there.

I studied the clouds. I must have looked skeptical because the man asked rather testily, "So, if there are flying saucers, why not flying lakes? Huh?"

# The Albatross

He lives in the wind. Always in flight, in the wind he sleeps.

He doesn't get winded or worn. And he's lived long; at the age of sixty he's still circling and circling the earth.

The wind warns him of storms and points the way to the coast. He never gets lost or forgets where he was born. But neither the earth nor the sea are his. On land he waddles on stubby legs, and in the water he soon grows bored.

When the wind deserts him, he waits. Now and then the wind might tarry, but it always returns. It seeks him out, calls to him, carries him off. And he lets himself go, lets himself fly, his great wings hovering in the air.

# The Sun Walker

Gustavo de Mello called me from the border. "Come on up," he said.

Don Félix was there. He was just getting in or just leaving, you could never tell which.

Neither could you tell his age. While we were putting away a bottle of red wine, he confessed he was ninety. Gustavo said he'd subtracted a year or two, but Félix Payrallo Carbajal had no birth certificate. "I never had any ID so I couldn't lose it," he told me while he lit another cigarette and blew a few smoke rings.

With no papers and no clothes beyond what he wore, he walked from country to country, from town to town, the length of the century and the breadth of the world.

Don Félix left sundials in his wake. Unlike most Uruguayans, who can't wait to retire, he still made his living that way. He built gnomons, clocks without mechanisms, and sold them in town squares. Not to tell time, a custom he considered discourteous, but for the simple pleasure of keeping the sun company on its earthly travels.

When we met in the city of Rivera, Don Félix was just starting to feel at home. That had him worried. The temptation to stay was an order to leave. "New, new, new!" he shrieked, banging the table with his childlike hands.

There, as everywhere else, he was just passing through. He came in order to leave. He arrived from a hundred countries and two hundred sundials, and he departed whenever he fell in love, fleeing the danger of setting down roots in any bed or abode.

For leaving, he preferred dawn. When the sun rose, he'd be on his way. As soon as the doors opened at the train or bus station, Don Félix would put the few bills he'd managed to save on the counter and say: "As far as this will take me."

# The Port

Grandma Raquel was blind when she died. But in Helena's dream, sometime later, Grandma could see.

In the dream, Grandma was no longer old nor a handful of tired bones. She was brand new, a four-year-old girl at the end of a voyage across the sea from far-off Bessarabia, one immigrant among many. On deck, Grandma asked Helena to pick her up, because the ship was docking and she wanted to see the port of Buenos Aires.

And in the dream, hoisted in her granddaughter's arms, blind Grandma saw the port of the country where she was to live the rest of her life.

# Immigrants a Century Ago

A lock of hair
a key that's lost its door
a pipe that's lost its mouth
a name embroidered on a handkerchief
a portrait in an oval frame
a blanket that used to be shared

and other things, big and small, lay wrapped among the clothes in the pilgrims' luggage. Not much room in a suitcase, but every suitcase contained a world. Beat up and bent out of shape, held together by rope or rusty latches, each one was alike but unlike any other.

The men and women, like their suitcases, were shunted from line to line, and like them they crowded together, in a heap, waiting. They came from tiny villages invisible on the map. At the end of the long crossing they had disembarked at Ellis Island, only a stone's throw from the Statue of Liberty, which, had arrived not long before they had, at the port of New York.

The island worked like a sieve. The gatekeepers of the Promised Land interrogated and classified the immigrants, listened to their hearts and lungs, studied their eyelids, mouths, and toes, weighed them, measured their blood pressure, temperature, height, and intelligence.

The intelligence tests were the hardest. Many of the new arrivals couldn't write and managed to mumble only a few unintelligible words in unknown languages. Among other questions they were asked how a staircase should be swept: Do you sweep from bottom to top, top to bottom, or toward the sides? A Polish girl answered, "I haven't come to this country to sweep staircases."

# The Years Soar

When autumn arrives, millions of butterflies begin their long voyage south, fleeing the cold of North America.

A river flows across the sky: soft fluttering waves of wings trace an orange splendor in the firmament as they fly. The butterflies cross mountains and plains and coasts and cities and deserts.

They are barely heavier than the air. During the twenty-five-hundred-mile journey, a few fall by the way, done in by exhaustion, wind, or rain. But the many who survive land at last in the forests of central Mexico.

There they discover the unseen kingdom that called them from afar.

They were born to make this flight. Later on, they return home. And in the North they die.

The following year, when autumn arrives, millions of butterflies begin their long voyage . . .

# Immigrants Today

Butterflies and swallows and flamingos have forever spread their wings to flee the cold, the way whales swim in search of other seas and salmon and trout seek out their rivers. Year after year, they all travel thousands of miles on the open roads of air and water.

The roads of human flight, however, are not free.

In immense caravans they march, fugitives fleeing their unbearable lives.

They travel from south to north and from rising sun to setting sun.

Their place in the world has been stolen. They've been stripped of their work and their land. Many flee wars, but many more ruinous wages and exhausted plots of land.

These pilgrims, shipwrecked by globalization, wander about, unearthing roads, seeking homes, knocking on doors that swing open when money calls but slam shut in their faces. Some manage to sneak in. Others arrive as corpses that the sea delivers to the forbidden shore, or as nameless bodies buried in the world they hoped to reach.

In forty countries, over several years, Sebastião Salgado photographed them. Three hundred portraits of this immense human tragedy amount to barely a second. The light that entered his camera for those pictures was barely a wink of the sun's eye, no more than an instant in the memory of time.

# The History That Might Have Been

Christopher Columbus couldn't discover America: he didn't have a visa or even a passport.

Pedro Álvares Cabral couldn't get of the boat in Brazil: he might have been carrying smallpox, measles, the flu, or other foreign plagues.

Hernán Cortés and Francisco Pizarro could never have begun the conquest of Mexico and Peru: they didn't have working papers.

Pedro de Alvarado was turned away from Guatemala, and Pedro de Valdivia couldn't enter Chile: they couldn't prove they had no police record.

The *Mayflower* pilgrims were sent back to sea from the coast of Massachusetts: the immigration quotas were full.

# Expulsion

In March of the year 2000, sixty Haitians put to sea in a leaky dinghy.

They all drowned.

Since this happens all the time, it didn't make the news.

The men swallowed by the waters of the Caribbean were all rice farmers.

They had fled in despair.

The rice farmers of Haiti have become raftsmen or beggars since the International Monetary Fund forbade government protection for local producers.

Now Haiti buys its rice from the United States, where the International Monetary Fund, which is rather absentminded, forgot to forbid government protection for local producers.

# Good-byes

Like a birthday but not a birthday. Beneath garlands of flowers and streamers, amid steaming cauldrons filled with corn dumplings, the devil in the bottles flowed freely and dancing feet raised a cloud of dust to the strains of guitars and quenas.

When the sun peeked in, a few guests were snoring in the corners.

Those still awake were saying good-bye to the man who was leaving. He was heading off with nothing but the clothes on his back and a passport from the Republic of Ecuador in his pocket. They gave him a woven blanket to brighten up his travels. He left by mule, and before long he vanished into the mountains.

He wasn't the first.

In town, only children and old folk remained.

Of those who left, not a one returned.

The guests stayed on to talk. "Such a wonderful fiesta! We cried so much!"

# Departure

A woman is heading north. She knows she might drown crossing the river or die crossing the desert from a bullet or thirst or snakebite.

She says good-bye to her children, wishing she could say see you later.

And just before leaving Oaxaca, at a little altar by the roadside, she kneels before the Virgin of Guadalupe and pleads for a miracle: "I'm not asking you to give. I'm asking you to put me where I can get for myself."

# Arrival

He set off walking from his village in Sierra Leone with no papers, with no money, with nothing. His mother sprinkled water on his footsteps to bring him luck on his voyage.

Of those who left with him, none arrived. Some were caught by the police; others were eaten by the sands or the sea. But he managed to reach Barcelona. Along with other survivors of other odysseys, he spends the night in Plaza Catalonia. He lies on the stone ground, face to the sky.

He looks for his stars. They aren't here.

He longs for sleep, but city lights never go out. Here night is also day.

# Ceremony

Stubby spent years behind the bar. He served drinks; sometimes he concocted new ones. He kept his mouth shut; sometimes he listened. He knew the quirks of all the regulars who came, night after night, to wet their whistles.

There was one guy who always showed up at the same time, eight o'clock on the dot, and ordered two glasses of dry white wine. He asked for two at once, and he drank them both, a sip from one glass, a sip from the other. In no hurry and in silence, he drained his two glasses, paid up, and took his leave.

Stubby had a rule: he never asked. But one night the fellow detected the curiosity in Stubby's eyes and, with a certain nonchalance, told the story. His closest friend, his lifelong buddy, had moved away. Tired of just scraping by, he'd left Uruguay behind and now lived in Canada.

"He's doing very well there."

Then, "I don't know if he's doing very well."

And then he clammed up.

Ever since his friend went away, the two of them met every night at eight on the dot Montevideo time, he in this bar, his friend in a bar there, and they had a drink together.

So it went, night after night.

Until the time the man came in, punctual as always, and ordered only one glass. He drank it slowly, silently, perhaps a bit more slowly and silently than usual, down to the last drop of that lone glass.

And when he paid the bill and got up to leave, Stubby did what he never does: he touched him. He stretched his arm across the bar and touched him. "My condolences," he said.

# Exile

Leonardo Rosiello came back from the northern reaches of the world. The trip from Stockholm to Montevideo did not go smoothly, there were problems with the connecting flights, and Leonardo arrived late at night when no one was expecting him.

At his parents' door he hesitated. "Shall I wake them or not?"

For years he had been living far away, a time of exile, the blind years under military dictatorship, and he was dying to see his family. But he decided it would be better to wait.

He set off down the street, the street of his childhood, and he was sure the pavement recognized his footsteps. His head filled up with old stories and bad jokes, and everything seemed fresh and delightful. It was a freezing winter night, the city cloaked in frost, but he savored the cold as if it were the tropics.

It took Leonardo a long while to realize he was carrying a suitcase, and that the suitcase weighed more than a tombstone. So he crossed the street, cut through an empty lot, and sat himself down on his suitcase, back to a wall.

The cold would not let him sleep. When he stood up, he could see in the moonlight that the wall was covered in scars: symbols and words, hearts pierced by arrows, vows of true love and angry oaths at love lost, even insults ("Maria has cellulitis").

Leonardo was also able to make out a few words that were nearly worn away, words that asked: "So where were you? What did you talk about? Who did you talk to?"

# Exiles

Some years had passed since the end of the Spanish War, but the vanquished still waged it every afternoon, arguing loudly in Montevideo's cafés. At night in the wine bars, commiserating over their defeat, they hugged each other as they sang songs from the trenches.

One of the exiles, who fought on the Republican front lines from the very beginning to the very end, recounted the entire war for me, blow by blow, at home in his kitchen. The battles took place on the tablecloth.

Teaspoons, sugar bowl, and coffee cups indicated the positions held by the militiamen and Franco's troops. A knife reared up and fired a shell that knocked over the bloodied pot of marmalade. Glasses—the tanks—rolled forward, crushing the toast with a crunch. Hitler's airplanes dropped oranges and rolls that shook the table and made mincemeat of the toothpicks, the infantry. At that breakfast table, my ears hurt from the thundering bombs, along with the roar of machine-gun fire, and the howls of the wounded.

# Time Weaves

She was five when she left.

She grew up in another country, spoke another language.

When she returned, she had lived a long life.

Felisa Ortega arrived in the city of Bilbao, climbed to the top of Mount Artxanda, and walked the path she never forgot, toward the house that had been hers.

Everything looked small, shrunken by the years. And she was afraid the neighbors would hear the drumbeat pounding in her breast.

She did not find her tricycle or the colored wicker chairs or the kitchen table where her mother, reading her stories, had with one snip cut out the wolf that made her cry. Neither did she find the balcony where they watched the German planes on their way to bomb Guernica.

Soon, the neighbors got up the courage to tell her: No, that wasn't her house. Her house had been destroyed. The one she was looking at was built on the ruins.

Then someone appeared from the depths of time. Someone who said, "I'm Elena."

They wore themselves out hugging each other.

They had played together so often in the groves of their childhood.

Elena said, "I have something for you."

And she brought out a white porcelain bowl with a blue pattern.

Felisa recognized the bowl her mother used for serving the hazelnut cookies she made for everyone.

Elena had found it unblemished amid the rubble and had saved it for fifty-eight years.

# The Foot

Many did not return. Of the citizens of the world who marched off to fight for the Spanish Republic, many stayed there, buried under Spanish soil.

Abe Osheroff of the Lincoln Brigade survived.

A bullet ruined one of his legs. With one foot dragging and the other foot walking, he returned to his country.

Spain was the first war he lost. From then on, carried by his roving foot, Abe never stopped.

Despite betrayals and defeats, beatings and jailings, he never stopped. One foot refused, but the other went right ahead. One foot told him, "I'm staying right here," but the other declared, "I'm taking you there." Time and again that foot, the errant one, hit the road, because dissent is destiny.

That foot carried Abe across the United States from end to end, from sea to sea, and it got him in repeated trouble, marching against McCarthy's witch hunts and the Korean War and racial segregation and the death penalty and the coup d'état in Iran and the crime of Guatemala and the butchery of Vietnam and the bloodbath of Indonesia and nuclear tests and the blockade of Cuba and the putsch in Chile and the strangling of Nicaragua and the invasion of Panama and the bombings of Iraq and Yugoslavia and Afghanistan and Iraq yet again . . .

Abe was ninety and still a marcher when his friend Tony Geist asked him, just out of curiosity, how he was doing. He raised his lion's head with its big white mane and smiled from ear to ear. "I'm still getting along, with one foot in the grave and the other one dancing."

# The Path of Jesus

Nailed by the palm of one hand, Jesus of Nazareth hung from what remained of a wall. The other Jesus, Jesús of Cambre, hung from a scaffold.

Jesús Babío, born in the center of Cambre, was a master bricklayer, master carpenter, master pipe fitter, and master blasphemer. Everything he did, he did well, but he'd been around and he knew that no one in the world could best him in the art of swearing, which like mysticism is a Spanish art. It was with pure streaks of blasphemy that Jesús, the one from Cambre, was rebuilding Santa María de Vigo church, burned by the reds during the war, while the other Jesus, the soot-blackened one from Nazareth, listened unamused.

"I shit on the hinges of the ciborium and on the nails of Christ and on his wounds and on his thorns, and I shit on the immaculate mother who birthed him."

Once in a while, Ángel Vásquez de la Cruz would ride into the ruined church on horseback. From high up on the scaffolding,

while hammering a wooden wedge or something, Jesús would tell him, between blasphemies, a story from his overseas travels. In his wanderings he had worked in England, Holland, Norway, Germany, even as foreign a place as Catalonia.

His stories all ended the same way. He'd point with his hammer at the empty window breached by the birds, and he'd point beyond to the path through Cambre's woods. No one would be coming down it, except maybe some local with a load of firewood on a mule. The path was just a bit of dirt among the trees.

"See that?" he'd ask. And he'd pass sentence: "I've walked down a lot of roads. I shit on the road to Calvary, I shit on the road to Santiago, and I shit on all highways. Everything there is to see in this world and the next goes by on that path right there."

# The Ants' Itinerary

The ants of the desert emerge from the deep and set out across the sand.

They search for food here and there, and in their wanderings they travel farther and farther from home.

Much later they return from a great distance, struggling to carry the food they found where there was nothing.

The desert makes a mockery of maps. The sand, swirled by the wind, never stays put. In that scorching immensity anyone can get lost. But the ants always take the shortest route home. They march in single file without hesitation, straight back to the spot from which they departed. Then they dig until they discover the tiny hole that leads to their nest. Never do they make a wrong turn, never do they enter someone else's hole.

No one understands how their little brains, weighing less than a milligram, can know so much.

# The Salmons' Way

Shortly after they're born, salmon abandon the river and head for the sea.

They spend their lives in distant waters until the day they begin the long return.

From the sea they climb the river. Guided by a secret compass, they swim against the current, leaping through rapids and over waterfalls, and they never stop. Many miles later they reach the spot where they were born.

The salmon return to give birth and die.

In the salt water they grew and changed color. Now they are enormous and not pale pink but reddish orange or silvery blue or greenish black.

Time has passed, and the salmon are not what they were. Nor is their birthplace. The transparent waters of their origin and destiny have become so murky that the bed of stones and boulders is hard to make out. But for millions of years they've believed that you can return, that round trips are not a lie.

# Poverty

Statistics say that the poor of the world are many, but in fact they are many more than the many they seem to be.

A young researcher, Catalina Álvarez Insúa, came up with a useful indicator to correct the calculations.

"Poor people are the ones they close the door on," she said.

When she defined her criteria, she was three years old. The best age for looking out at the world and seeing.

# The Closed Door

From the far-flung villages of El Gran Tunal, Pedro and his burro Shorty set out for Mexico City.

Pedro walked more than he rode to give Shorty's tired back a break. Both of them were getting on in years and the journey was long.

Walking the days away, they finally reached the grand plaza, the Zócalo. And they planted themselves at the door to the National Palace, where power resides.

There they remained, waiting for an audience. Pedro and Shorty had come to relate what was happening back home, and to demand justice. Corralled on land of stone and dust that offered a steady diet of dust and stone, the Indians of El Gran Tunal were extinct, officially, and did not even figure in the statistics. Out there justice was farther away than the moon, since the moon at least was visible.

There was no getting rid of Pedro and Shorty. Whenever they were chased from the plaza, they'd come right back. Nothing worked, not niceties, not nightsticks. Shorty would put on his donkey's face and Pedro a face that said, you're-wasting-your-time, we've-been-at-this-for-five-hundred-years.

At the end of 1997, at the age of eighty-seven, nearly dead from breathing the poisoned air of Mexico City, Pedro got an injection, the first of his life. Unmovable, he stayed camped out, while Shorty turned a deaf ear to the insults of the press, who called him a "means of transport."

Pedro and Shorty lived in the open at the door of the National Palace for one year, two months, and two weeks. Then they headed home.

The door never opened, but these two obstinate souls managed to achieve something: their people were no longer invisible.

Soon after the punishing walk back home, Shorty died, perhaps of humiliation: he had learned that power was an even bigger ass than he was. Now he shares a cloud in the heavens with Emiliano Zapata's white horse.

# A Lesson in Law

The poor of endless indigence are waiting in line.

The law gets up early. Today a lawyer will see people first thing.

He notices an elderly woman waiting with a slew of kids and a baby in her arms. When her turn comes, she shows him her papers. The children aren't her grandchildren; this woman is thirty years old, and the nine children are her own.

She has come to ask for help. She built a tin and wood shack somewhere on the slopes of the Cerro slum in Montevideo. She thought the land belonged to no one, but it belonged to someone. And now they're going to boot her out. She is facing the thing they call eviction.

The lawyer listens. He examines the papers she has brought.

They've no right, thinks the specialist in rights. He shakes his head, takes a long while to speak. He swallows, lowers his eyes, and says, "I'm sorry, ma'am, but . . . nothing can be done."

When he looks up, he sees that the eldest daughter, a little girl with the face of a ghost, has her hands over her ears.

# A Lesson in Medicine

Rubén Omar Sosa heard about Maximiliana's lesson during a course on intensive care in Buenos Aires. Of all the things he learned in his years as a student, this was the most important.

A professor recounted the case history: Doña Maximiliana, worn out by the burdens of a life without Sundays, had been in the hospital for several days, and every day she asked: "Please, Doctor, could you take my pulse?"

A slight pressure of the fingers on the wrist, and he'd say, "Very good. Seventy-eight. Perfect."

"Yes, Doctor, thank you. Now, would you please take my pulse?" And he'd do it again and explain again that everything was fine, couldn't be better.

Day after day, the same scene. Whenever he went near Doña Maximiliana's bed, that voice, that ragged wheeze called and held out the twig of an arm, over and over and then yet again.

He played along because a good doctor should be patient with his patients, but he thought, "This old bird is a pain in the neck." And he thought, "She's got a screw loose."

It took him years to realize she was asking for someone to touch her.

# Maternity

Tertuliana Queiroz waits somewhere in Ceará.

She waits, her children wait.

She had fifteen.

She left one newborn at the church door. She traded a grown daughter for a cow.

In better times, she talked a blue streak. Now she stutters.

Eight left, she says.

She counts with her fingers, whispers names. No, she says, seven.

The others are dead—died or killed.

She looks to the heavens with the eyes of a sleepwalker.

God called them, she says.

So it goes.

# Mother's Day

In the mail I receive a brochure promoting a special offer for that special day. The finest gifts for the self-sacrificing woman who gave you life. "Sleep well at night," the brochure promises, and for a reasonable price it suggests remote control alarms, handheld sirens, electronic high-tech keys, impenetrable window guards, security cameras, triple-lens infrared sensors, and magnetic trips for doors and gates.

# The Latest Fashion

The new century's style is on display in Bogotá at Miguel Caballero's establishment for haute couture.

This young company is the most successful fashion firm in the country. It sells a lot, here and overseas, and earns a lot of money and a lot of envy.

"In my line of work, there's no margin for error," explains the proprietor as he tests a new line by firing a pistol at one of his employees.

Fear is no longer naked. In the service of public security and personal elegance, Caballero produces armored clothing.

His impenetrable items are protected by a synthetic fiber five times stronger than steel. He offers a variety of weights and designs: two-pound T-shirts, four-pound raincoats, coats in leather or camel hair, party dresses, sports clothes, vests festooned with hearts . . .

# Clues

Nobody knows whether it happened centuries ago or yesterday or never.

A woodsman went out to work and discovered his ax was missing. He looked at his neighbor and saw a typical ax thief: the face, the gestures, the way of speaking . . .

A few days later, the woodsman found his ax lying right where he had left it.

And when he looked at his neighbor again, he saw nothing like a typical ax thief, neither the face, nor the gestures, nor the manner of speaking.

# Evidence

"Good evening," the deep voice begins, and goes on to announce the worst: "Fear, impotence, helplessness . . ."

Mixing television's favorite cocktail of blood and panic, TV Globo shocks millions of Brazilians with the savage deeds of a sub-human criminal class against the defenseless public.

In August 1999, their sights are trained on Marcos Capeta, terror of Bahía and heir to the legendary Cangaceiro bandits.

Professional actors dramatize the scene. The opening shot shows the astonished faces of the police. Then, we see the beast point his machine gun, which fires two thousand rounds a minute at three times the speed of sound, and the police cruiser explodes. There's no skimping on special effects: flames dance across the murderer's smiling cynical face.

Television is judge and jury. Without hearing a word from Marcos Capeta, the small screen sentences him to die. It won't be easy. Capeta's gang is vast.

A spectacular manhunt is launched. The forces of order take charge of the execution.

In the following episode, the screen serves up the prize. The audience breathes a sigh of relief and breaks into applause. After a long and arduous battle, society has one enemy less.

Nilo Batista takes the trouble to read the DA's file and the police report. The outlaw was gunned down in an isolated house. He had no machine gun, never had one, and his gang consisted of a fourteen-year-old boy, who died at his side.

# The Declaration

"Tell us the facts as you know them," the judge orders.

The court reporter, fingers on the keyboard, takes down the response of the accused, aka the Screw, resident of the city of Melo, age, eighteen; marital status, single; profession, unemployed.

The accused doesn't deny responsibility for the crime he's alleged to have committed. Yes, he strangled a chicken that did not belong to him. "I had to kill it," he declares. "My empty stomach had been grumbling for too long."

And he concludes, "Judge, it was self-defense."

# The Sentence

We were out chasing wine, empanadas, and songs with Perro Santillán, Diablero Arias, and some other friends, when somebody invited Petete, who was deceased, and he joined us for a few drinks.

I'd never met him before, but during our midday binge the pudgy little man and I became friends. He told me he had died because, poor though he was, he had the truly awful thought to get sick. He went into a diabetic coma in the middle of the night, and the Jujuy hospital had no insulin.

233

# The Prison

In 1984, sent by a human rights organization, Luis Niño visited the prison yards of Lurigancho Penitentiary in Lima.

Luis plunged into a lonely sea of half-naked, ragged prisoners and barely managed to elbow his way through.

Afterward, he asked to speak with the warden. The warden wasn't in. The chief of medical services received him.

Luis said some of the prisoners were dying, spitting up blood, and many more were burning with fever and covered in sores. And he hadn't seen a single doctor. The chief explained, "We doctors only come in when the nurses call us."

"So why don't they call you?"

"We don't have the budget for nurses."

# The Execution

The electric chair was first used on July 30, 1888.

That day the city of New York, always in the vanguard of world progress, did away with the barbaric practice of the gallows and the hooded executioner. Civilization inaugurated an immediate, scientific, foolproof, and pain-free death.

An audience was invited to witness the event.

The prisoner, gagged and bound with heavy belts, received a three-hundred-volt shock. He writhed and moaned but did not die.

They cranked up the generator and gave him four hundred volts. More violent spasms. Still alive.

When they let him have seven hundred volts, his snout exploded in a spurt of foaming blood, and a faint, throaty howl was heard.

The fourth shot did him in.

The prisoner was a dog named Dash.

He had been convicted, without evidence, of biting two people in the street.

# Poor Man's Funeral

According to those in the know, Evilweed got his name from hiding in the greenery, disguised as a tree to fool the Mexican police.

Some say the bandit, who always gave away his loot, never actually lived, but no one denies that he exists. Though he's no Vatican saint, he has a shrine in Culiacán, a few steps from the government palace. The government promises miracles. Evilweed performs them.

Pilgrims come to the shrine from the hills and the coast to leave gifts of gratitude: the husk of the first corn from my harvest, my first shrimp of the season, the bullet that did not kill me.

Limes sit on the altar in a row. Each of the faithful takes one. Taken alone, limes cleanse the mouth. Taken in faith, they cleanse the soul and bring good luck.

The shrine stands on the spot where Evilweed fell when they gunned him down. That was many years ago. The funeral was forbidden, and that's what started the hail of stones. People came from all around to throw them. The authorities were pleased to see the people stone the bandit. A tall pyramid of stones covered Evilweed.

Under the guise of punishment, the people built him a home.

# Buried in Style

Airplane pilot Jorge Aguilar inhabits in a three-story vault, bathed in eternal light. Behind polarized glass, eagle wings pay homage to his skill and to the memory of this martyr of free trade.

The six-column parthenon of Lobito Retamoza sees no darkness either, illuminated as it is by solar energy.

Dr. Antonio Fonseca, gunned down on the streets of Guadalajara along with his wife and bodyguards, lies in a vast phosphorescent crypt, surrounded by huge images of his loved ones and a color portrait of a pensive Jesus Christ.

Filled with light and marble angels and plastic toys, the sepulchre of the little children of Güero Palma commemorates the innocents who were dropped from a great height in an act of unjustified vengeance.

The drug traffickers and their families reside in a luxurious section of the Culiacán cemetery, Humaya Gardens. All their monuments feature telephones just in case they ever revive.

Their birthday parties last several days and nights with bands that play round the clock to accompany the drinking. The parties take place without incident. Only once did shots ring out, but that was because one of the musicians, claiming exhaustion, refused to keep playing.

"Since then, the orchestras keep their side of the deal," explains Ernesto Beltrán, groundskeeper and gravedigger, while he picks up the empties.

# Discipline

The British jurist and philosopher Jeremy Bentham invented a moral calculus that allowed him to measure Good and Evil.

To combat Evil, he created the perfect prison in 1787. He called it Panopticon. It was a large cylinder of cells, laid out in a ring around a central tower. From the tower, the watchman kept watch, while those being watched could not see the watchman watching them. The penitentiary design could also be used as an asylum, a factory, a barracks, or a school.

Over the years, many countries put this architecture of power into practice intended, as it was, for "punishing the incorrigible, guarding the insane, reforming the vicious, confining the suspected, employing the idle."

When he died, Bentham received his last wish. He had his body stuffed and seated in his usual chair, dressed in black, his cane in his fist. Thus for years to come the tamer of the world's chaos could continue to watch over the meetings of the board of trustees of the University College of London. "Present but not voting," as it was noted in the minutes.

# The Evil One

In Colombia, the hired hands call him Don Sata. He gives them machetes that cut sugarcane on their own, hands-free. He goes drinking with them, and all have a grand time, with not the slightest whiff of sulphur or fear of getting scorched.

In Bolivia, the miners call him Uncle. In exchange for cigarettes and liquor he leads them through the bowels of the mountains and shows them the very best veins.

In Argentina, the north belongs to him during carnival. But on Ash Wednesday, the possessed are dispossessed; they bury the lord of the fiesta, he who never drinks water, and they bid him a tearful farewell until next year.

At parties in Brazil's crowded slums, they sound their drums to call this special guest, infamous avenger of the humble. They beg him to do them the disfavor of coming to live in the world, which is just like Hell only the climate is better.

# The Good One

José María Escrivá de Balaguer, who watches out for us from Heaven, is a saint, practically an angel.

In life, this pious servant of God preached love of war, denounced reds and libertines, hated homosexuals and Jews, scorned women, and founded Opus Dei.

Long before the pope made him a saint, Generalísimo Francisco Franco made him a marquis, in compensation for his services. While Franco went about exterminating the Spanish Republic and annihilating heretics, Escrivá sang hymns of praise and tended to the state of his spirit.

Along the path to divine grace, he worked many miracles.

His most astonishing miracles occurred in 1996. Escrivá was deceased by then and not yet a saint, though he was getting close, and from Heaven he came to the aid of victims of common crime. In Guadalupe, Mexico, one follower begged his little Escrivá medal for help, and the very next day his stolen pickup was found. A short while later, several of the faithful prayed a novena in Milan, Italy, and six stolen cars, the latest-model luxury sedans, were miraculously recovered by their owners.

# A Pro

He was the foundation of his home, his mother's cane, his sisters' shield.

Deep within his house, at the end of a long corridor, was an altar to the Virgin. There, he plucked his bullets, duly prayed over, from a bowl of holy water and tied the scapular to his breast, before heading out to do a job. The mother and sisters remained before the altar on their knees, counting rosaries hour after hour, bead after bead, pleading with the Miraculous One to lend the young man a hand.

His professional skills won him fame and respect in the streets of Corinto and in other towns and cities of the Cauca Valley. His reputation did not spread to all Colombia, only because the competition was fierce.

He lived by plugging people, and he died being plugged.

Except for the four bullets for his wife, which were his own affair, he always killed for hire. He pulled the trigger for businessmen, generals, heirs, and husbands.

"Don't get me wrong," he'd say. "I do it for the money."

# Another Pro

At the end of every month, General Arturo Durazo, chief of the Mexico police, collected the wages of two thousand officers who had died or never been born. He also charged a commission for every gram of cocaine or heroin that passed through the country, and anyone who played forgetful paid with his wares or his life. To round out his revenue, the man responsible for public safety also sold positions on the force: it cost a million and a half pesos to become a colonel, but for his favorite singers he gave out captains' stripes as gifts.

In 1982 he received an honorary doctorate, and the papers published a picture of him dressed in cap and gown.

By then, with savings from a lifetime of dedication, General Durazo managed to achieve the dream of owning his own home. Actually he owned several, in Mexico and around the world. Of his Mexican estates, one featured furniture from France, another had an English racetrack and a New York discotheque, a third was a faux chalet from the Alps, and where would he be without an exact replica of the Parthenon, complete with swimming pool?

He ended up in jail for the crime of exaggeration.

# How to Succeed in Life

In 1999, according to the *Times of India*, a new educational institution was finding great success in the city of Muzaffarnagar, in the western part of the state of Uttar Pradesh.

The school specialized in skills training for teenagers. The educator Susheel Mooch taught the most advanced course, which covered, among other topics, kidnapping, extortion, and execution. The two other directors took care of more conventional subjects. All the courses included fieldwork. For example, to master highway robbery, the students learned to crouch out of sight and throw a metal object at a car. When the impact startled the driver into stopping, they would proceed to rob him—under the professor's supervision, of course.

The school emerged in response to clear market demand, and it fulfills a useful social function. As those in charge explained, the market insists on ever higher degrees of specialization in the field of crime, and criminal education is the only professional training that guarantees young people a shot at well-paid permanent employment.

# Beggars

To succeed in life, even beggars need an education.

From glimpses of television in bars and store windows, they learn pointers from the masters of the craft: Latin America's presidents, who pass the hat at international conferences and practice the art of pleading during their periodic pilgrimages to Washington.

That's how beggars are inspired to embroider their pitch. A pro never asks for spare change for a drink. Never. He puts his hand out for a few bucks to take his mother to the hospital or to buy the casket for the child he just lost, waving all the while the prescription or the death certificate in his other hand.

From the small screen, beggars also learn to give something in return. Their country is the street, so they have no lands or mineral rights or state companies to offer. But they can repay charity with a reserved seat in the Great Beyond: "Don't make me steal, Jesus also begged, the Bible says so, may God repay you, may God hold you in his Glory, you'll go to Heaven for sure . . ."

# Work Clothes

One hundred and thirty-five years after his death, Abraham Lincoln was spotted on the streets of Baltimore, Annapolis, and other cities in Maryland.

Lincoln would walk into a store, any store. Touching the brim of his top hat, he'd make a slight bow. Then, stroking his graying beard without mustache, he'd survey the panorama with his unmistakable, mournful eyes, and from his black frock coat he'd pull a Magnum 357. In his direct style, that of a man who never beats around the bush, he'd say, "Your money or your life."

During the month of May in the year 2000, Kevin Gibson, dressed as Abraham Lincoln, held up eleven stores before the police caught him.

Gibson will be in prison for quite a while. He wonders why. After all, don't the country's most successful politicians don Lincoln's mantle to do precisely the same?

# The Robber Gets Robbed

Under the military in Latin America, they burned books. Under democracy, they cook them. Military dictatorships disappeared people. Financial dictatorships disappear money.

One fine day Argentina's banks refused to give account holders their money.

Norberto Roglich always kept his savings in the bank so they wouldn't get eaten by mice or stolen by thieves. When he got robbed by the bank, Don Norberto was quite ill—years take their toll—and his meager pension fell short of his medical bills.

He had no choice. He marched into the financial fortress and without asking anyone's permission went straight to the manager's desk. In his fist he gripped a grenade. "Give me my money, or I'll blow us all to kingdom come."

The grenade was a toy, but it worked a miracle. The bank gave him his money.

Later on, Don Norberto got arrested. The prosecution asked for eight to sixteen years. For him, not the bank.

# The Cop Gets Busted

Playing teacher's pet, doing whatever she was told, Argentina sold off everything, even the lions in the zoo and the paving stones from the sidewalks, and still she owed a candle to every saint. At the beginning of 2003, the International Monetary Fund and the World Bank, which had done so much to gut the country, sent a mission to look over the books.

One of the members of this financial swat team, Jorge Baca Campodónico, was in charge of tax evasion. An expert on the topic he was, having often committed it himself. Interpol grabbed him as soon as he landed in Buenos Aires.

There was a warrant out for that one.

Not for his bosses.

# Word Thieves

According to today's dictionary, "good stock" is not proud lineage but a firm whose price is on the rise, and it's in the stock market where "values" get undermined.

The "market" is no longer that beloved neighborhood spot for buying fruit and vegetables. Now "Market" is a frightful and faceless lord, who sees all, claims to be eternal, and does not hesitate to punish. His oracles say, "The Market is nervous," and they warn, "We mustn't upset the Market."

The "international community" is the name of the big bankers and their warrior chiefs. Their "aid packages" sell leaden lifesavers to the countries they drown, and their "peace missions" pacify the dead.

In the United States, the Ministry of War is called the "Defense Department," and "humanitarian bombing" is the name for the downpour of missiles they rain on the world.

On a wall, written by someone, written by everyone, I read: "My voice aches."

# Muggings

While words lose their meaning, the sea and sky lose their color, the green and blue they were painted through the kindness of algae giving oxygen for three billion years.

And the night loses its stars. Protest signs have been seen in the world's great cities: "They won't let us see the stars." Signed: "The people."

And in the firmament, there are banners crying: "They don't let us see the people." Signed: "The stars."

# It Happens All the Time

Advanced in years, Doña Chila Monti hovered on the border between Earth and Heaven, closer to the harp than the guitar.

Her son Horacio knew it, but it was still a shock when he saw her eyes rolling, her heart fluttering, and her hands all atremble. With the bit of breath she could muster, Doña Chila managed to mutter, "I've been robbed."

Horacio asked which of her things had been stolen, and instantly her vision, her breathing, and her steady hand returned. As did her tongue. Indignant, she said, "Things? You know I don't have anything. What could they take? When God calls me, I'll go with nothing but the clothes on my back."

And she spelled it out: "Not things. The crooks stole my ideas."

# Memory Stolen

In 1921 the peons of Patagonia went on strike. The estate owners called the British ambassador, who called the Argentine president, who called the army.

Firing Mausers, the army put down the strike and the strikers too. The peons were pitched into common graves on the estates, and at shearing time no one who knew how to shear the sheep was still alive.

Captain Pedro Viñas Ibarra commanded the operation at one estate. Half a century later, by which time the captain was a retired colonel, Osvaldo Bayer spoke with him. He got the official story. "Oh, yes," the officer recalled "Anita Estate. That battle."

Bayer wanted to know why that battle had left six hundred workers dead and not a single soldier killed, wounded, or even scratched.

And the armed wing of order kindly explained: "The wind. We were upwind. That's why our bullets flew true. Their shots into the wind went awry."

# Memory Bought

In 1839 the U.S. ambassador to Honduras, John Lloyd Stephens, bought the Mayan city of Copán, gods and all, for fifty dollars.

In 1892, near New York, an Iroquois chief sold four sacred belts that his people had held forever. Like the ruins rising from the weeds of Copán, those seashell belts related a people's history. General Henry B. Carrington bought them for seventy-five dollars.

In 1937, to whiten the Dominican Republic, General Rafael Leónidas Trujillo murdered eighteen thousand blacks, all Haitians, just like his own mother's mother. Trujillo paid the Haitian government twenty-nine dollars a head in reparations.

In the year 2001, following several trials for his crimes, Chilean General Augusto Pinochet paid a fine of $3,500. A dollar for every person killed.

# Memory Burned

In 1499, in the bonfires of the Inquisition, Archbishop Cisneros of Granada put the torch to books that preserved eight centuries of Islamic culture and thirteen centuries of Jewish culture in Spain.

In 1562, in the Yucatan, Fray Diego de Landa condemned eight centuries of Mayan literature to the flames.

Elsewhere in the world, other conflagrations had occurred before and many occurred thereafter, memories consumed by fire.

In the year 2003, when the invading army completed its conquest of Iraq, they surrounded the oil wells, oil depots, and Oil Ministry with tanks and troops. Soldiers whistled and looked the other way, however, when the museums were sacked and the books of fired clay that recounted the first fables, the first stories, the first written laws in the world were pillaged.

Next, Baghdad's National Library went up in smoke, and half a million books were reduced to ashes. Many of the earliest publications in Arabic and Persian, died there.

# Traditions

He was his family's headache, the worst student in his class. The disgrace had no solution, until the father of that wretched student put on a banquet for his teacher. At the end of a long evening of food and flattery to delight his pride and palate, the teacher went home weighed down with gifts. By morning, the worst student had become the best.

A word more, a word less, this story from over four thousand years ago has never gone out of style, proving that bribery is one of Civilization's oldest customs.

It was found on the banks of the Euphrates. The Sumerians told it, through symbols that look like bird tracks drawn with pointed canes on one of the thousands of clay tablets that disappeared from the Baghdad Museum.

# The Pioneer

Humanity's Great Inventions: No one knows who invented the wheel that moves carts and machines, but we know who invented the wheel that drives the economy. It was Marco Licinio Craso, born 115 years before Christ.

He discovered that the market depends on the push and pull of supply and demand for goods and services.

To put this economic law into practice, he founded a company in Rome.

Thus was born the first private firefighting firm.

It was a great success.

Don Marco set fires, then charged to put them out.

# Another Pioneer

Pepe Arias founded the first virtual company. Half a century before online commerce and NASDAQ, he put four thousand square feet of land up for sale in Buenos Aires.

Pepe greeted prospective buyers, contract in hand, ready for the signing. He received them on his feet, because the place wouldn't even hold a chair.

"Where is the land?" they asked.

"Here."

"Here?"

"Yes, sir," Pepe explained, raising his arms to the heavens. "Four thousand square feet, straight up."

# Role Models

When the end of the millennium was drawing near, our local press touted a huge success story. It was about a Uruguayan who shone with his own light in Internet heaven. As it turned out, the glow from our star of cyberspace was rather fleeting, but while it lasted the president of the country exhorted us all to follow his example.

This exemplary entrepreneur had been a child prodigy. At the age of six, he rented out toys to his friends in the neighborhood, at daily or hourly rates. By the time he was ten, he had founded an insurance company and a bank: he insured school supplies against theft or accident and lent his schoolmates pocket change at a reasonable rate of interest.

# State of the Art

Levi Freisztav came to Patagonia nearly half a century ago.

He came out of curiosity or maybe by happenstance. Strolling through the land, breathing in the air, he realized his parents had chosen the wrong map. And he stayed for good.

When he first came south, he found work on a hydroponics project. A local doctor had read about the novel idea and decided to give it a try.

Levi dug, hammered, and sweated day after day, knocking together a complicated structure of glass, metal struts, and split pipes for growing lettuce in water. If they do it in the United States, the doctor liked to say, it's a sure thing; those people are the vanguard of civilization, technology is the key to wealth, we're centuries behind, and we'd better run if we're going to catch up.

Back then, Levi was still a man from an asphalt world, the type who believes tomatoes grow on dinner plates and who goes bug-eyed when he sees a chicken uncooked and walking. But one day, contemplating the immensities of Patagonia, it occurred to him to ask, "Listen, doc. Is it worth it? Is it worth it, with so much land to be had?"

That was the end of his job.

# On Sale

He looked like Carlos Gardel, after the plane crash. He coughed, adjusted the knot in the scarf protecting his throat. That rag had once been white.

"I'm not selling anything!" he growled.

He was standing on a bench across from the Pensioners Credit Union in Montevideo. In his hands he held a cardboard box, tied with bits of string as frayed as he was.

A few onlookers gathered, all of them elderly or very elderly. Pepe Barrientos, who was always wandering about the city, stuck his nose in too. Gradually, the onlookers became a crowd.

"I'm not selling anything!" the man repeated.

When the moment arrived, he raised the box with a theatrical gesture and offered it to the heavens. "Ladies and gentlemen, I'm not selling anything! Because this . . . this is priceless!"

The old folks pressed in anxiously, while those bony fingers, moving as parsimoniously as a lover prolonging his pleasure, slowly untied the twine that held the mystery fast.

The box opened.

Inside were pieces of colored cellophane tied in the shape of butterflies.

Each cellophane was a new life. They were green, blue, purple, red, yellow . . .

"Your choice!" the crier growled. "Pay what you can and get a new life! It's a gift, ladies and gentlemen! You'll pay more for a bottle of wine that contains poison, prison, insanity!"

# Marketing

Salim Harari always kept a little bag of pepper, that unfailing weapon of the East, close at hand to throw in the eyes of thieves. But not even thieves bothered to come in. The store, La Lindalinda, was as empty as the stomachs of his nine children.

Salim had come from far-off Damascus to sell fabric in the town of Rafaela. He wasn't about to give up. The lemon tree wouldn't bear fruit, so he tied lemons to the branches. Not a single customer came in, so from the balcony he tossed yards and yards of cloth into the street. "We're giving it all away!"

News arrived that a ship had sunk in the Paraná River, so he sprayed water on his satins, calicos, and taffeta and shouted, "Cloth rescued from the shipwreck!"

Even that failed. It was useless. People walked by and looked the other way.

His misfortune lasted a long time. Every day was worse than the last and better than the next, until one night Salim rubbed a burned-out lamp and a genie from the old country appeared. The genie divulged the magic secret: charge to get in.

That's when Salim's luck turned. The entire town lined up.

# The Exemplary Banker

John Pierpont Morgan Jr. owned the most powerful bank in the world, as well as eighty-eight other companies. Since he was a very busy man, he forgot to pay his taxes.

When the story broke, he'd been remiss for three years running, ever since the crash of '29. The many who had been ruined by the catastrophe on Wall Street were furious, and it became a national scandal.

To alter his rapacious image, the banker turned to the head of public relations for Ringling Brothers Circus.

The PR man suggested he hire a phenomenon of nature, Lya Graf, a thirty-year-old woman who stood twenty-seven inches tall but had neither the face nor the body of a dwarf.

A huge publicity campaign was launched, built around a photograph of the banker on his throne, gazing like a kind father at the miniature woman on his knee. The symbol of financial power sheltering the common people who had been diminished by the Depression. That was the idea.

It didn't work.

# A Class in Political Economics

The sound of the organ announced the wafer man's arrival in our neighborhood. Made of wheat and air, and of music too, those crusty wafers made our mouths water.

The number of wafers was a matter of luck. For a coin, you'd spin a dial until the needle came to rest on your lucky number: from zero to twenty, if I remember right. You'd end up with either nothing, a little, a lot, or a banquet.

I'll never forget my first time. I handed over my coin, reared up on my tiptoes, and spun the dial. When it stopped, I saw the needle pointing at twenty. Then the wafer man stuck in his finger and decreed, "Zero."

I protested, in vain.

I could count to twenty with the help of both hands, but I didn't know a darned thing about political economics.

That was my first lesson.

# The Exemplary Worker

Potion Z might sound like a high-tech concoction from the era of the globalized labor market, but it is an ancient Haitian secret.

Here is how it works:

At night, bees raised on Potion Z ram their stingers under the skin of an innocent sleeper.

At dawn, the inoculated victim can't get up.

At noon, he goes out like a candle.

At dusk, his loved ones carry him on their shoulders to the cemetery.

At midnight, the deceased opens his tomb and returns to the world.

The returnee, a zombie, will have lost his passion and his memory. He will work all day at no pay, grinding cane or raising walls or carrying wood, his eyes a blank, his mouth clamped shut. He will never complain or demand a thing. He won't even ask.

# The Exemplary Woman

She lived in obedience to God and Tradition.

She swept, polished, lathered, rinsed, ironed, sewed, and cooked.

At eight on the dot she served breakfast, with a spoonful of honey for her husband's eternal sore throat. At twelve on the dot she served dinner: consommé, mashed potatoes, boiled chicken, peaches in syrup. And at eight on the dot supper, the menu unchanged.

She was never late, never early. She ate in silence, voicing neither questions nor opinions, while her husband recounted his exploits present and past.

After supper, she took her time washing the dishes and later crept under the covers praying to God he was asleep.

By then the washing machine, the vacuum cleaner, and the female orgasm, all of which had arrived shortly after penicillin, were fairly common, but she never heard the news.

She only listened to soap operas on the radio and rarely left the sanctuary of peace that kept her safe from the violence of the world.

One afternoon she went out to visit a sister who was ill.

When she returned at dusk, her husband was on the floor, dead.

Several years later, this woman confessed that the story hadn't ended exactly like that.

She told the other ending to a neighbor named Gerardo Mendive, who recounted it to his neighbor, who in turn told it to yet another, who then passed it on again. When she returned from her sister's, she found her husband on the floor, trembling, panting, cross-eyed, beet-red. She walked on by into the kitchen, where she prepared a sumptuous feast of squid in its ink and hake à la Basque, with a tower of fruit and ice cream, over which she poured a vintage wine she kept hidden. And at eight on the dot, as was her duty, she served supper, ate and drank her fill, then confirmed he was still on the floor and definitely not moving. She crossed herself, put on her black dress, picked up the phone, and called the doctor.

265

# The Exemplary Athlete

Two world soccer championships were held in Asia in the year 2002. One was played by athletes of flesh and blood, the other, at the same time, by robots.

World robot tournaments take place in a different city every year. Their organizers hope someday to compete against human players. After all, they say, a computer defeated Gary Kasparov on the chessboard, and it doesn't take much to imagine mechanical athletes achieving a similar feat on the soccer field.

The robots, programmed by software engineers, are powerful on defense and quick on the attack. They never tire or complain. They carry out the coach's orders without kidding around, and not for an instant do they ever entertain the lunacy that players are supposed to play. And they never laugh.

# Coronation

Correction: not two, but three. In 2002 there was also a third World Cup.

It was a single match, played amid the peaks of the Himalayas on the same day that Brazil was crowned champion in Tokyo.

No one heard about it.

The contest was between the two worst teams on the planet, last and next-to-last in world rankings: the kingdom of Bhutan and the Caribbean isle of Montserrat.

The trophy, a great silver-plated cup, waited at the edge of the field.

The players, none famous, all anonymous, with no duty but to enjoy themselves, had a grand time. At the end of the match, the cup, glued down the middle, was split in two and shared by both teams.

Bhutan won and Montserrat lost, but that detail didn't matter in the least.

# The Exemplary Mourner

In one way they are all alike. In Brazil and everywhere else, eminent politicians, soccer idols, TV stars, popular musicians, and all other celebrities have one thing in common: they are all mortal.

Jaime Sabino took careful note of this. And every time someone famous met his fate, Jaime was first to find out and first to turn up. No matter where the funeral was held, Jaime, who worked as a lowly clerk in a government office on the outskirts of Rio de Janeiro, would drop everything and be there at the speed of light.

"I come representing the two hundred thousand inhabitants of Nilópolis," he would say, and thus move smoothly past all checkpoints and security barriers. Anyone can stop a man alone, but no one can deny entry to two hundred thousand.

Instantly, Jaime would find the right spot at the right time.

Just when the TV cameras started rolling and the photographers' flashes lit up the air, he'd heft the casket holding the glory that left behind a vacuum impossible to fill, or he'd appear among the family and closest friends, on tiptoe straining to see. His stricken expression was always featured in the coverage on TV and in magazines and the papers.

Reporters called him "the pirate's parrot." Out of envy.

# The Dead Woman Who Worked Miracles

Living is a fatal habit; nobody gets around that. Even Doña Asunción Gutiérrez died, after a long century of life.

Relatives and neighbors held the wake at her home in Managua. The wailing had long since died down and tears had given way to drinks and laughter when, at the height of the evening, Doña Asunción sat up in the casket.

"Get me out of here, you idiots," she ordered.

Then she tucked into a tamale, without so much as a nod to anyone.

The mourners slipped silently out. Stories no longer had anyone to tell them; cards had no one to play them; the drinks had lost their pretext. A wake without a body just won't do. Everyone disappeared up the dirt streets uncertain what to do with what remained of the night.

One of the great-grandchildren grumbled, "This is the third time the old bag does this to us."

# Inflation

He'd been skinny all his life, but in death he was a blimp.

To get the lid of the casket nailed down, the entire extended family had to sit on it. A diversity of opinions emerged regarding his sudden spread.

"Death makes you swell."

"It's the carbonic gas."

"It's his rotten moods."

"It's his soul," sobbed the widow. "His soul is trying to get out of that suit."

The suit, an English tweed, was the only luxury the dead man had ever allowed himself. When owls were hovering near and the end was in sight, he had it made to measure, so at least he could clothe his death in something.

He left no inheritance. Nothing. The family had always lived in poverty and detected no change.

Many years later, Nicola Di Sábato attended her uncle's exhumation.

Not much was left of the body, just bones and the suit in tatters.

The suit was stuffed full of money.

The bills, many thousands of them, were by then worthless.

# The Exemplary Candidate

He did not cry when evoking his underprivileged childhood. He did not kiss babies or sign autographs or have his picture taken alongside invalids. He did not promise a thing. He did not inflict interminable speeches on the voters. He made no proposals from the left or the right or the center. He couldn't be bribed; he turned up his nose at money, although bouquets of flowers made him smack his lips loudly.

In the 1996 elections, he topped all polls. He was the leading candidate for mayor in the town of Pilar, and his fame spread across Brazil's Northeast. Tired of politicians who lie even when they tell the truth, people trusted this young even-toed ungulate bovine, commonly known as a goat, who was white with a beard to match. At rallies, Federico danced on his hind legs and frolicked persuasively to the beat of the band that accompanied him on his campaign stops.

On the eve of certain victory, he was found dead, his beard red with dried blood. Poisoned.

# The Ballot and the Bullet

It was 1916, an election year in Argentina.

In the town of Campana, people voted at the back of the general store.

José Gelman, a carpenter by profession, was the first to arrive. He was going to vote for the first time in his life, and his breast swelled with civic pride. That morning this immigrant, who had come from the other side of the world, who had never known anything but the despotism of military rule in Ukraine, was about to join the democratic process.

When José went to place his vote in the ballot box, a vote for the Radical Party, a hoarse growl stayed his hand. "You picked from the wrong pile," the voice warned.

Through the window grate he spied the barrel of a shotgun. The barrel gestured toward the correct one, the pile of ballots for the Conservative Party.

# The Price of Democracy

Doris Haddock, a retired worker, walked from Los Angeles to Washington, D.C. A tortoise crossed the United States from coast to coast.

She set out to decry the selling of democracy to the millionaires who finance political campaigns, and she gave speeches all along the way.

She'd been on the march for over a year, fried by the sun, frozen by the cold, blown by the wind, when she got stopped by the snow. An enormous snowfall covered the state of Virginia.

Doris celebrated her birthday in the town of Cumberland. Ninety candles. And she pressed on by ski.

For the entire last month, she skied through the snow.

She reached Washington for the birth of the twenty-first century. A large crowd accompanied her to the Capitol, workplace of the hired hands who sell their legislative services to the highest corporate bidder.

On the steps of Congress, Doris made a laconic address. Pointing at the Capitol doorway, she said, "This is turning into a bawdy house."

And she walked away.

# Civilization and Barbarism

While the gods sleep, or pretend to, people walk. It is market day in this town hidden on the outskirts of Totonicapán, and there is a lot of coming and going. From other villages, women carrying bundles arrive by verdant pathways. Like teeth seeking a mouth, they meet up in this market today, tomorrow in another, and they catch up on everything by chatting leisurely as they sell one thing at a time.

An old woman spreads her cloth on the ground and lays out her wares: copal incense, anil and cochineal dyes, a few very hot chiles, herbs for cooking, a bowl of wild honey, a rag doll, a doll made of painted clay, belts, laces, sashes, necklaces made of seeds, combs made of bone, little mirrors . . .

A tourist, new to Guatemala, wants to buy it all.

Since she does not understand, the tourist says it with his hands: *everything.* She shakes her head. He insists, "Tell me what you want, and I'll tell you what I'll pay." And he repeats, "I'll buy *everything.*" His voice grows louder. He yells. She, a seated statue, remains silent.

The tourist, fed up, storms off. He thinks, "This country is never going anywhere."

She watches him go. She thinks, "My things don't want to go with you."

# The World Market

Trees the color of cinnamon, fruit of gold.

Mahogany hands wrap white seeds inside large green leaves.

The seeds ferment in the sun. Later, unwrapped and in the open, the sun dries them and slowly paints them copper.

Then, cacao begins its voyage across the blue sea.

Between the hands that grow it and the mouths that eat it, cacao is processed in factories owned by Cadbury, Mars, Nestlé, or Hershey and is sold in the supermarkets of the world. For every dollar in the cash register, three and a half cents go to the villages from which cacao comes.

A journalist from Toronto, Richard Swift, was in one of those villages in the mountains of Ghana.

He visited the plantations.

When he sat down to rest, he pulled a few chocolate bars from his pack. Before he could take a bite, he was surrounded by curious children.

Here was something they had never tasted. They loved it.

# The Global Government

At the dusk of the twentieth century and of his own life, Julius Nyerere spoke with the international community. That is to say, he got an audience with the big shots at the World Bank in Washington.

Nyerere became Tanzania's first president following a long struggle against the colonial power, and he believed in independence and wanted it to be much more than a salute to the flag.

"How come you failed?" the top international experts asked him.

Nyerere answered, "We took over a country with eighty-five percent of its adult population illiterate. The British ruled us for forty-three years. When they left, there were two trained engineers and twelve doctors. This is the country we inherited. When I stepped down, there was ninety-one percent literacy and nearly every child was in school. We trained thousands of engineers and doctors and teachers. For the last ten years, Tanzania has been signing on the dotted line and doing everything the IMF and the World Bank wanted. Enrollment in school has plummeted to sixty-three percent, and conditions in health and other social services have deteriorated."

And Julius Nyerere returned the question: "How come you failed?"

# The White Man's Burden

Captain Leon Rom collected butterflies and human heads. The butterflies he pinned to the wall. The heads decorated his garden. Another officer of the colonial army, Guillaume Van Kerckhoven, competed with him and claimed to be the champion head chopper.

The Congo, a hundred times the size of Belgium, was the personal property of King Leopold. A prodigious source of rubber and ivory, it was also an immense tableau of slaves enchained, flogged, mutilated, murdered.

In the year 1900, the British diplomat Roger Casement was invited to dine at the Royal Palace in Brussels. Between courses, King Leopold spoke of his mission to spread civilization and the tremendous difficulties it faced at every step. An especially huge challenge was imposing discipline on an inferior race that ignored the culture of work, especially under an African sun hot enough to melt stones.

The king acknowledged that at times his men, men of goodwill, mind you, committed abuses. The climate was to blame. "The heat is intolerable. It drives them crazy."

# The Wonders of Science

At the age of twenty-six, he went under the knife for the first time.

From that point on, he lived between the operating room and the stage.

What color is the world's summit? The color of snow. To become king of kings, tallest of the tall, he changed his skin, his nose, his lips, his eyebrows, and his hair. He painted his black skin white, sharpened his broad nose, his thick lips, and his bushy eyebrows, and sowed his scalp with straight hair.

Thanks to the chemical industry and the art of surgery, twenty years of injection after injection, operation after operation, cleansed his appearance of African damnation. Not a single stain remained. Science had defeated nature.

By then, his skin was the color of the dead, his much mutilated nose was a splotchy slice, his eyebrows were a picture of fright, and his head sported a wig.

None of him was left. Only his name. He continued calling himself Michael Jackson.

# The Wonders of Bureaucracy

Sonia Pie de Dandré gets up early because her job requires it and also because she likes to breathe in the newborn day when it smells like a baby.

That morning she hummed softly as she walked through Santo Domingo's streets moist with new light, and she was among the first in line at the counter to pick up her passport. When she got it, she saw that the description included her skin color. "Brown," the passport said.

Sonia is black and sees nothing wrong with that. She asked them to correct the error. Error?

"In this country, there are no blacks," said the clerk, also black, who had filled out the forms.

# Incantations

Alexandra Schjelderup came back from the cold.

She had spent fifteen years living far away.

The first thing Alexandra did when she arrived was turn on the radio. She wanted to hear the news and the voices of her country, Panama, which owes a debt to the Indians for the tamales that make her mouth water, for the hammock where she sleeps her floating siestas, for the colors she flaunts and the memories she suppresses.

The radio was playing an ad with a phone call cutting in and out, unintelligible sounds, followed by a woman asking furiously, "Who is this Indian calling me?" A businesslike voice then advised, "If you don't want to be mistaken for an Indian, get your Cable & Wireless cell phone now."

# The Little Christ

The Girl Mary slept little or not at all. From the moment light peeked out from between the mountains until the end of every evening, the Girl Mary was on her knees before the altar, whispering her prayers.

At the center of the altar reigned a small brown Christ. The little Christ, darkened by incessant candle smoke, had human hair, black, from the local people. The peasants of Conlara Valley often visited that child of God, who looked so much like them.

The Girl Mary lived in poverty and filth, but every day she bathed the little Christ in springwater, covered him with flowers from the valley, and lit the tapers surrounding him. She never married. In her pretty years, she'd cared for her two deaf-mute brothers. After that, she dedicated her life to the little Christ. Her days were spent taking care of his home, and at night she watched over his sleep.

In exchange for so much, the Girl Mary never asked for a thing.

Then at the age of one hundred and three, she asked. She didn't name the favor, but she voiced her promise. "If you come through, little Christ," she said, "I'll dye your hair blond."

## Blessed Healer

The doctor had no secretary, and I don't believe he had a telephone either. His office, with neither Muzak nor carpet nor Gauguin prints on the walls, had nothing but a cot, two chairs, a table, and a diploma from the medical school.

He managed to become the most miraculous healer in Boca neighborhood. This man of science cured people without pills or herbs or anything at all. Dressed in a housecoat, he'd begin by asking, "So, what disease would you like to have?"

# Blessed Remedy

Two centuries ago, in the city of Salvador de Bahía, the loftier families summoned as many doctors as they could afford to circle the deathbed.

Relatives and neighbors piled into the bedroom to listen. After examining the patient, each physician offered a lecture on the case. These were solemn speeches, and the audience commented in lively tones:

"I support that!"

"No! No!"

"Well done!"

"The doctor's wrong!"

"Agreed!"

"What horseshit!"

Once the first round was over, the specialists took the floor again to explain their points of view.

The debate grew long. But not very long. Even the toughest of the moribund would hurry his last breath along, even if it was in bad taste to interrupt the work of Science.

# Another Blessed Remedy

In America, nobody planted coconuts. Coconuts planted themselves. The first one broke free from some tree in Malaysia, rolled across the sand, and was carried out with the current. Floating on the seven seas, the errant coconut reached the coasts of America. It liked these beaches and has offered us its healing juices ever since.

Andrea Díaz was jogging one afternoon at the edge of the Pacific when she felt she'd lost her knees. Somebody took her to the port of Quepos and gave her coconut water.

"Drink this," he ordered.

And he explained there was no better remedy. "Adam and Eve never drank anything else, and they never caught a single disease."

She obeyed, but she couldn't help asking, "How do you know that?"

The man gave her a look filled with pity. "Child, it's in the Bible. Don't you see? There were no doctors in Paradise. Disease came after doctors."

# Miracles

On the last bend in the rue Mouffetard in Paris, I found the church of Saint Médard.

I opened the door and went in. It was Sunday afternoon. The church was empty; the echoes of the last noon prayers had faded away. There was a cleaning woman sweeping up after mass, dusting saints, but nobody else.

I went through the church from stem to stern. In the dim light, I was searching for the royal ordinance from the year 1732: "By order of the King, God is prohibited from working miracles in this place."

Carlitos Machado had told me the prohibition was carved in a stone at the entrance to this church, which was dedicated to a saint too free and easy with miracles. I looked, but I did not find.

"Oh, no sir! No! Absolutely not!" The cleaning woman, armed with a broom and wearing a helmet of curlers, grew indignant yet continued working without looking up.

"But that order of the king's . . . was it ever here?"

The cleaning woman faced me. "Was it? It was. But not anymore."

She rested her hands on the tip of the broomstick and her chin on her hands. "That sort of thing didn't set the right tone for the believers. You understand."

# I Give Thanks for the Miracle

Beside the altar in Mexican churches, ex-votos proliferate. They are images and words painted on small pieces of tin that give *thanks to the Virgin of Guadalupe, because Pancho Villa's troops raped my sister and not me;*

*thanks to the Blessed Child of Atocha, because I have three sisters and I'm the ugliest and I got married first;*

*thanks to the Little Virgin of Sorrows, because the night before last my wife took off with my buddy Anselmo and now he's gonna pay for all the things he did to me;*

*thanks to the Divine Face of Acapulco, cause I kilt my husband and they dint do nothin to me.*

That's the way it was. And still is. But you also see novelties, like ex-votos that give *thanks to Our Lord Jesus Christ because I crossed the river and came to the Unite Estays and I didn't go under or get died.*

Alfredo Vilchis, better known as Leonardo da Vilchis, paints on commission in the market at La Lagunilla. The Christs in his little paintings all have his face. And to accompany the words of thanks, he often paints archangels dressed as soccer players. Many of his clients made promises to Heaven before decisive matches, and the divine hand bestowed the grace of goals on their beloved club or on the Mexican national team.

# The Great Beyond

At the end of the southern summer of '96, José Luis Chilavert scored a memorable goal in Buenos Aires. The Paraguayan keeper, who was great at blocking goals and also at scoring, shot from afar, practically from the center of the field. The ball flew up through the clouds into the heavens, then dropped straight down into the opposing net.

Journalists wanted to know how he did it. What was the secret of that kick? How did he make the ball take that incredible journey? How could it fall in a straight line from such a height?

"It hit an angel," Chilavert explained.

But no one thought to check the ball for bloodstains. Nobody bothered to look. And so we lost a chance to find out if angels are like us, if only in that way.

# The Virgin

The past as macho exploit: no women figure in the official history of the Canary Islands.

None? There is one.

She arrived centuries ago on the coast of Tenerife, long before Spain conquered the islands.

She floated in on the waves, asleep in the foam, and was picked up by fishermen. When they spoke to her, she did not answer. The fishermen took her to the king of the island. She remained mute before the monarch. And when the princes killed each other quarreling for her favor, she observed the spectacle without batting an eye.

The only woman in the official history of the islands is still there. Her name is Mary, and they call her Candelaria, for the tapers that illuminate her. She is a virgin and is made of wood. Men worship her on their knees.

# The Others

The Gospel according to Saint Matthew says Jesus had forty-six ancestors: forty-one men and five women.

One of the five women, everyone knows, conceived without sin. But the others in his lineage were: Tamar, who dressed up as a prostitute so she could have a child with her father-in-law; Rahab, who plied the oldest trade in the city of Jericho; Batsheva, who was married to another when she begat Solomon in King David's bed; and Ruth, who was not of the chosen people and was thus not deemed worthy of the faith of Israel.

Three sinners and one scorned. The damned of the earth were the grandmothers of the son of Heaven.

# Christmas Eve

Spain. December 24 to 25, 1939.

"It's Christmas Eve. We'll get some sort of present," said Javier, and he chuckled to himself.

Javier and Antón, prisoners of Franco's troops, were traveling with their hands tied behind their backs. The jolting of the truck threw them against each other, and every so often the soldiers jabbed them with their bayonets.

Javier talked nonstop. Antón kept quiet.

"Where are they taking us?" asked Javier, who was really asking, Why me, why me, I'm not a red, I'm no troublemaker, I never got involved, I'm not political, not at all, never, not me, not ever, nothing.

On one of the bumps in the road, they ended up face-to-face, eye-to-eye, and then Javier squeezed his eyelids shut and muttered, "Antón, listen. It was me."

But they couldn't hear a thing over the roar of the truck. Nearly screaming, Javier repeated, It was me, it was me. "I brought them. It was me."

Antón stared at the side of the road. There was no moon, but the forests of Asturias were glowing. Javier said they forced him; they had his entire family on their knees; they were going to kill them, the children, everyone. Antón was still off in the woods that shone in the darkness with their own light, a radiance that flowed up against the truck.

Javier fell silent.

There was only the coughing of the motor and the grinding of the truck on the road.

After a moment, Javier repeated, "It's Christmas Eve."

And he said, "It's so cold."

The truck stopped. A firing squad was waiting.

# Easter Sunday

Nineteen seventy-three. Montevideo, Ninth Cavalry barracks. A rotten night. Roar of trucks and machine-gun fire, prisoners facedown on the floor, hands behind their heads, a gun at every back, shouts, kicks, rifle blows, threats . . .

In the morning, one of the prisoners who hadn't yet lost track of the calendar recalled, "Today is Easter Sunday."

Gatherings were not allowed.

But they pulled it off. In the middle of the yard, they came together.

The non-Christians helped. Several of them kept an eye on the barred gates and an ear out for the guards' footsteps. Others walked about, forming a human ring around the celebrants.

Miguel Brun whispered a few words. He evoked the resurrection of Jesus, which promised redemption for all captives. Jesus had been persecuted, jailed, tormented, and murdered, but one Sunday, a Sunday like this one, he made the walls creak and crumble so there would be freedom in every prison and company in every solitude.

The prisoners had nothing. No bread, no wine, not even cups. It was a communion of empty hands.

Miguel made an offering to the one who had offered himself. "Eat," he whispered. "This is his body."

And the Christians raised their hands to their lips and ate the invisible bread.

"Drink. This is his blood."

And they raised the nonexistent cup and drank the invisible wine.

# The History of Fear

The moon had something to say to the earth and sent a beetle with the news.

The beetle had been en route through the sky for several million years, when he met up with a hare.

"You'll never get there at that pace," the hare warned, and he offered to take the message himself.

The beetle handed over his mission: "Tell the women and the men that the moon says, 'Like the moon gets reborn, so will you.'"

And the hare, running with the fleetness of a hare, set off for Earth.

Rather sooner than later, he landed in the jungle of southern Africa, where people lived in those days, and without pausing to catch his breath he passed on the moon's words. The hare, who is always leaving even before he arrives, spoke in his usual headlong way. And the women and the men understood him to say, "The moon gets reborn, not you."

Ever since, we have been doomed to suffer the fear of dying, which is the father of all fears.

# The Art of Ruling

An emperor of China—no one knows his name or his dynasty or his epoch—summoned his principal adviser one night and confided the anguish that would not let him sleep. "No one fears me," he said.

Since his subjects weren't afraid of him, they did not respect him. Since they did not respect him, they did not obey him.

"It takes punishment," the adviser suggested.

The emperor said he had already ordered anyone who failed to pay tribute to be whipped, anyone who did not bow when he passed to be tortured slowly, and anyone who dared criticize his decisions to be sent to the gallows.

"But those are the guilty," the adviser said. And he explained: "Power without fear deflates like a lung without air. If you punish only the guilty, only the guilty feel afraid."

The emperor meditated in silence and said, "I understand."

He ordered the executioner to cut off the adviser's head, and he commanded the entire population of Beijing to witness the spectacle in the Plaza of Celestial Power.

The adviser was first on a long list.

# The Anatomy of Fear

The day is born, touched by the sun's fingers.

In the countryside of El Salvador, women light fires and begin their chores.

"How did you dawn?" they ask, because, like the day, they dawn.

And by their bodies they know what the new day will bring.

During the war years, every woman's body at dawn was a map of fear. If fear pressed against her breasts, one of her sons would not return. A sharp pain in the belly meant the army was approaching. And if her kidneys ached, there would not be enough water in the well and she would have to risk their lives searching for more.

# Fright

The river nearly swallowed her.

Eufrosina Martínez was washing clothes when the current caught her and dragged her downstream. After a lot of flailing about among the rocks, she managed to save herself, but she lost her soul. The fright took it. Her soul, scared stiff, sank and vanished from sight.

After that, the soulless body of Eufrosina could not move or eat or sleep or distinguish night from day.

A healer from the mountains of Puebla cured her. Her soul returned from fear and rejoined her body. Then Eufrosina rose and walked once more on this earth that sometimes snatches your feet from under you, like an angry river.

# The Bogeyman

Playing nonstop, everybody thrown in together, the kids lived in a joyous scramble of bugs, children, and plants.

But one awful day, some wanderer reached that tail end of nowhere in the expanses of Paysandú and brought fear.

"Watch out, the bogeyman's coming!"

"The bogeyman is coming to take you away!"

"The bogeyman is coming to eat you up!"

Olga Hughes noticed the first symptoms of the plague. A sickness that no pharmacy can cure began to afflict her numerous children. And that's when she chose from among her many dogs the tamest and friendliest one, and baptized him Bogeyman.

# The Magic Flute

Through the streets wandered the healer of tools that had lost their edge.

The sharpener's foot spun the emery wheel and pulled showers of sparks from the blades of knives, razors, scissors. We neighborhood kids, a swarm of admirers, were the audience for the show.

Just as the organ announced the wafer man, the flute was the crier for the sharpener.

People said if you were thinking about something and heard the sound of that flute, you changed your mind on the spot.

Practically no sharpeners remain on the streets of cities; the whistle of their flutes no longer drifts in through open windows. Other songs resound instead, tunes of trepidation, airs of alarm, and many are the people who change their minds in a flash.

# The Plague

The ship glided south along the Swedish coast on a calm sea.

It was a splendid summer morning. The passengers sat on deck enjoying the sun and the soft breeze, waiting for breakfast.

Suddenly, a girl ran to the railing and threw up.

Then the woman beside her did the same. Immediately, two men got up and followed suit. One after another, the rest of the passengers seated in the bow also vomited.

Those seated on the poop deck laughed at the ridiculous spectacle, but soon a few of them were leaning out over the calm sea and putting their fingers down their throats, and others followed.

No one could keep from vomiting.

Victor Klemperer was in one of the seats farthest aft. To keep from joining the retch-fest, he concentrated on the meal to come: coffee with cream, orange marmalade . . .

Then the passengers in the stern had their turn. Every one of them threw up. He did too.

Klemperer forgot about this incident. It came back to him a few years later in Germany, during Hitler's unstoppable ascent.

# Red Alert

The country no one invades, and has the habit of invading others, is terrified of being invaded.

In the eighties, the threat was called Nicaragua. President Ronald Reagan fumigated public opinion with toxic clouds of fear. When he went on TV to decry the danger, a red tide flowed across the map projected behind him. A torrent of blood and communism spread from Central America, washed over Mexico, and penetrated the United States through Texas.

The TV audience hadn't a clue where Nicaragua was. Nor did they know it was a barefoot country flattened by half a century of dictatorship manufactured in Washington, and by an earthquake that erased much of the city of Managua from the map.

The fount of fear had a total of five elevators, plus an escalator that wasn't working.

# The Opinion Mill

It was the year 1964, and the dragon of international communism spread all seven of its maws wide-open to devour Chile alive.

Ads bombarded public opinion with images of burned-out churches, concentration camps, Russian tanks, a Berlin wall in downtown Santiago, and bearded guerrillas carting off children.

Elections were held.

Fear triumphed.

Salvador Allende was defeated.

During those painful days, I asked him what hurt the most. And Allende told me what had happened right over there, at his neighbor's house in the barrio of Providencia. The woman who broke her back working there as cook, maid, and nanny in return for a pittance, put all the clothes she owned in a plastic bag and buried it in her bosses' backyard. So the enemies of private property couldn't take them from her.

# The Hooded Man

Six years later, bucking the tide of fear, the left won Chile's elections.

"We cannot allow . . . ," warned Henry Kissinger.

At the end of a thousand days, the military bombarded the presidential palace, pushed Salvador Allende to his death, executed many more, and saved democracy by murdering it.

In the city of Santiago, the soccer stadium was turned into a prison.

Thousands of detainees sat in the stands, waiting to learn their fate.

A hooded man moved among them. No one saw his face, but he saw everyone. His gaze fired bullets. A repentant ex-socialist, the hooded man walked, paused, and pointed. The men he marked, who had been his mates, marched off to torture or death.

The soldiers led him by a rope around his neck.

"That guy looks like a dog," said the prisoners.

"But he isn't," said the dogs.

# The Professor

Outside, a noise of boots with spurs. Somewhere far above the heights of his boots thundered the voice of Paraguay's police chief Alcibíades Britez, a servant of the fatherland who collected the salaries and received the rations of all deceased policemen.

Naked, lying facedown in a puddle of his own blood, the prisoner recognized the voice. This was not his first visit to hell. Every time students or landless peasants raised a stink, every time the city of Asunción woke up blanketed with leaflets evincing little affection for the military dictatorship, they would interrogate him, strapping him to the machine for grinding human flesh.

The boot kicked him, turned him over. And the chief's voice passed sentence. "Professor Bernal . . . you ought to be ashamed of yourself. Look at the example you're setting for young people. Professors aren't there to make trouble. Professors are there to make citizens."

"That's what I do," stammered Bernal.

He answered by a miracle. He was but the remains of himself.

# The Windmill

Nelly Delluci crossed barbed-wire fences and pastures looking for a concentration camp called the Little School, but the Argentine army had left not a brick standing.

All afternoon she wandered about, searching in vain. When she was lost as could be in the middle of an open field, Nelly spied the windmill. She saw it in the distance. As she approached, she heard the creaking of the sails in the wind and she was certain.

"It was here."

There was nothing but grass around her, but this was the place. Standing in front of the windmill, Nelly recognized the sound that fifteen years before had kept her and the rest of the prisoners company, day after day, night after night, while torture ground them to bits.

And she remembered that a colonel, fed up with the windmill's unceasing complaints, ordered it handcuffed. Rope was looped several times around the sails to hold them fast. The windmill kept moaning.

# Echoes

He got out, but he stayed behind. Fray Tito was free, in exile in France, but he remained imprisoned in Brazil. His friends confirmed what the maps told him, that the country of his executioners lay on the far side of the ocean, but that did not help. He was the country where his executioners lived.

He relived his hell every day. Everything that had happened, happened all over again. For more than three years, his torturers never let up. Wherever he was, in the convents of Paris and Lyon, or in the countryside of southern France, they kicked him in the stomach and cracked him across the head with their rifle butts, they stubbed out cigarettes on his naked body, and stuck cattle prods in his ears and mouth.

And they never shut up. Fray Tito was bereft of silence. In vain he wandered in search of some place, some corner of the church or the earth free of the horrible screams that would not let him sleep, would not let him say the prayers that had once been his magnet for God.

He could not go on. "Better to die than to lose your life" were the last words he wrote.

# The Keeper

At noon, in a beer hall on the docks of Hamburg, two men were drinking and talking. One was Philip Agee, the former CIA station chief in Uruguay. The other was me.

The sun, not a very frequent visitor to those latitudes, bathed the table in light.

Between beers, I asked him about the fire. Years before, *Época*, the newspaper where I worked, had gone up in flames. I wanted to know if that had been a little present from the CIA.

No, Agee told me. The fire was a gift of Divine Providence. And he added, "They gave us a fabulous ink for incinerating printing presses, but we didn't get the chance to use it."

The CIA failed to place a single agent in our print room. The foreman, Agee acknowledged, was "a great goalkeeper."

Yes, I said. He was.

Gerardo Gatti, with that chronic and incurable smile in his eyes. Yes, he was a great keeper. And he also knew how to attack.

When Agee and I met in Hamburg, Agee had broken with the CIA, a military dictatorship was governing Uruguay, and Gerardo had long since been kidnapped, tortured, murdered, and disappeared.

# Losses

In Guatemala, under the military dictatorship, the daughter of Don Francisco was captured in the Chuacús Mountains. Before dawn, an army officer dragged her to her father's door.

The officer interrogated Don Francisco. "Is it wrong what the guerrillas are doing?"

"Yes. It's wrong."

"And what should be done with them?"

Don Francisco did not answer.

"Should they be killed?" the officer demanded.

Don Francisco remained silent, his eyes on the ground.

His daughter was on her knees, hooded, handcuffed, a pistol at her head.

"Should they be killed?" the officer insisted.

Again and again. Don Francisco still said nothing.

Before the bullet shattered the girl's skull, she wept. Under the hood, she wept.

Carlos Beristain told me this story. "She wept for him," he said.

# Absences

Death wears a thousand colors in the cemetery of Chichicaste-nango. Perhaps these flowering tombs celebrate the end of the earthly nightmare, this bad dream of bullies and bullied which ceases when death, in one blow, strips us naked and makes us all equals.

I don't see a single headstone from 1982 or 1983, the time of the great killings in the indigenous communities of Guatemala. The army threw those bodies into the sea, or into the mouths of volcanoes, or burned them in who knows what common graves.

The joyful colors of the tombs of Chichicastenango salute death, the Equalizer, who treats beggar and king with the same courtesy. Missing from the cemetery are those who died for wanting life to do the same.

# Encounters

He hadn't been at the factory long before a machine bit his hand. A thread had got away, and in his attempt to catch it he got caught.

He didn't learn. Héctor Rodríguez spent his entire life reaching for dropped threads, organizing unions, gathering the dispersed. Throughout his years on the blacklist and his years in jail, he risked his hand and everything else to weave together what fear had unraveled.

When his days came to an end, a large group of us waited for him at the cemetery gate. Héctor was to be buried on the hill above Buceo Beach. We'd been there quite a while on that gray and windy day, when several cemetery workers turned up carrying a casket but without flowers or mourners. A number of us who had been waiting for Héctor formed a cortege behind them and went in.

By mistake? Did we follow the wrong casket? Who knows? It would have been just like Héctor to offer his friends to the one who was all alone.

# The Door

Carlos Fasano spent six years conversing with a mouse and with the door of cell number 282.

The mouse wasn't very faithful, scurrying in and out at will, but the door was always there.

Later on, the prison was turned into a shopping center. From lock-up to buy-up; its cells no longer held people but Armani suits, Dior perfumes, and Panasonic VCRs.

The doors ended up in a junkyard.

There, Carlos found his door. It had no number, but he recognized it straightaway. Those were the gashes he'd made with his spoon. Those were the old stains in the wood, maps of secret countries he traveled to during each of the long days he spent in confinement.

Now the door stands in the open, at the top of a hill, where closing is forbidden.

# Memory

He fought, was wounded, got caught.

After the torture chamber, he was pretty much dead when a military court decided he should die altogether.

He knew he was alone. What remained of him had been forgotten by his comrades.

Utterly forsaken, he waited for death to finish the job.

In the solitude of his cell, he talked to the wall.

But the end of the war got there before death did, and he was set free.

In the streets of San Salvador, he continued talking to walls, and he punched them with his fists and hit them with his head because they would not answer.

He ended up in an asylum. There, they kept him tied to a bed. He no longer spoke, not even to the walls.

Norma, who years before had been his friend, went to see him. They untied him. She gave him an apple. Without a word, he gazed at the apple in his hands, that red and luminous world, and soon began slicing it with his teeth. Then he got up and handed out the pieces, bed by bed, to all the rest.

That's how Norma learned: "Luis is crazy, but he's still Luis."

# *Tik*

In the summer of 1972, Carlos Lenkersdorf heard this word for the first time.

He had been invited to an assembly of Tzetzal Indians in the town of Bachajón, and he did not understand a thing. He was unfamiliar with the language, and to him the heated discussion sounded like crazy rain.

The word *tik* came through the downpour. Everyone said it, repeated it—*tik*, *tik*, *tik*—and its pitter-patter rose above the torrent of voices. It was an assembly in the key of *tik*.

Carlos had been around, and he knew that in all languages *I* is the word used most often. *Tik*, the word that shines at the heart of the sayings and doings of these Mayan communities, means "we."

# The Hummingbird

In certain villages lost in the Andes, those with long memories recall the time the sky sat on the world.

The sky was so low that people went about stooped over and couldn't straighten up without banging their heads. Birds would take off and crash into the roof at the first flap of their wings. The eagle and the condor charged with all their might, but the sky paid no heed.

The crush ended when a tiny dancing bolt of lightning flashed through the little air that remained. It was the hummingbird, and he stuck the sky's behind with his needlelike beak. He kept stabbing away, obliging it to rise higher and higher until it reached the heights where it now stands.

The eagle and the condor symbolize strength and flight. But it was the smallest of the birds that liberated the earth from the weight of the sky.

# Sex Symbol

The flea doesn't flaunt. He doesn't erect masts, towers, obelisks, or skyscrapers. Nor does he churn out rifles, cannons, or missiles.

The he-flea, lover of the she-flea, has no need for faux phalli. He's got the real thing. It extends a full third of the length of his body, a size bested by none in the entire animal kingdom. And to top it off, it's covered in down.

For thousands of years, the bullies and butchers of the human species have kept this humiliating fact secret.

# The Lion and the Hyena

The lion, emblem of bravery and nobility, invigorates anthems, dignifies flags, and stands guard over castles and cities. The hyena, symbol of cowardice and cruelty, neither invigorates nor dignifies nor guards anything. Leo the lion offers his name to kings and plebeians, but no one has ever been named Hyena.

The lion is a carnivorous mammal of the Feline family. The male specializes in roaring. His females hunt deer, zebras, and other defenseless or distracted beasts, while the male awaits his dinner. When the meal is ready, the male eats first. Whatever is left is for the females. Then, if anything at all remains, the cubs eat. If nothing is left, they do without.

The hyena, a carnivorous mammal of the Hyaenidae family, has other habits. He is a gentleman who brings the food and eats last, after the children and ladies have served themselves.

To praise, we say, "He's a lion." And to insult, "He's a hyena." The hyena laughs. I wonder why.

# The Bat

He got his bad reputation from Count Dracula.

Batman tried to improve his image, but the bat still arouses more terror than gratitude.

This symbol of the kingdom of darkness does not fly through the night in search of human necks. In real life, the bat does us the favor of fighting malaria by hunting a thousand mosquitoes an hour and is kind enough to help farmers by devouring harmful pests.

Despite our calumnies, this efficient pesticide does not give us cancer or charge so much as a cent for his services.

# The Shark

In movies and books, the cunning and bloodthirsty monster navigates the seven seas with jaws spread wide to reveal his teeth of a thousand knives. He dreams of us and licks his lips.

Outside movies and books, the shark fails to show the slightest interest in human flesh. Rarely does he attack us, and then only in self-defense or by mistake. When a nearsighted shark confuses one of us with a dolphin or a seal, he takes a bite and spits it out. We're a lot of bones and not much meat, and our not-much-meat tastes awful.

We are the dangerous ones, and sharks know it. But sharks don't make films or write novels.

# The Rooster

The famous rooster of Morón was neither a herald nor a symbol of the new day.

He was, so they say, the judge or the tax collector or the king's envoy. Gallo, meaning "rooster," was his name, and he'd strut about town proclaiming, "Wherever this cock crows, everyone else shuts up."

Adulator and humiliator, he licked up and spit down.

For years the silenced remained silent, until one fine day they attacked the ornate little town hall from which he perpetrated his abuse. They caught the malefactor, tore off his clothes, and chased him naked through the streets under a shower of stones.

This happened, so they say, some five centuries ago in the Spanish city of Morón de la Frontera, where visitors can still observe the defeathered fowl in full flight, sculpted in bronze. It's a warning: tread carefully, you who are drunk with power or even a little tipsy; you too could end up plucked and squawking and driven from the city.

# The Hen

A look at the facts from Veterinarians Without Borders and from the U.S. Air Force shows that hens and warplanes don't have much in common.

The hen looks like a hen and is called Hen, while a B-2A warplane looks like a bat and is called Spirit.

A hen costs at most five or six dollars, while each plane costs $2.2 billion.

A hen in good shape can cover half a mile, while the plane can fly 6,900 miles at twice the speed of sound without refueling.

The hen can't fly much more than a hand's breadth off the ground, while the plane flies at over thirty thousand feet.

The hen lays an egg a day, while the plane lays eighteen tons of satellite-guided bombs.

# Doves

Sylvia Murninkas was rollerblading along Montevideo's water-front on a calm afternoon filled with light, when she heard the tumult of war.

The fighting was in the Hotel Rambla, which was undergoing renovations. The ground floor was filled with debris, and on top of the broken bricks and splintered wood lay a carpet of white feathers.

Sylvia backed away in fright. The symbols of peace were hacking each other to pieces with their beaks. They threw themselves at each other in sudden bursts, spun around in the air, crashed against the windows, then returned, bathed in blood, to the battle.

# Heroes

From afar, presidents and generals give the order to kill.

They won't fight, except with their wives.

They won't shed blood, except when they nick themselves shaving.

They won't breathe poison gas, except for what cars spit out.

They won't sink in the mud, no matter how much it rains in their backyards.

They won't vomit from the stench of bodies rotting in the sun, only from the occasional spoiled hamburger.

They won't be deafened by the bombs that blow people and cities to pieces, only by the fireworks at the victory celebration.

They won't be kept awake by the eyes of their victims.

# The Warrior

In 1991 the United States, which had just invaded Panama, invaded Iraq because Iraq had invaded Kuwait.

Timothy McVeigh was programmed to kill. In basic training, they ordered him to scream, "Blood makes the grass grow!"

Pursuing that ecological end, they showered the map of Iraq in blood. Planes dropped enough bombs to make five Hiroshimas, then tanks buried the wounded alive. Sergeant McVeigh crushed quite a few amid the sand dunes. Enemies in uniform, enemies with none. "They're collateral damage," he was told to say.

He won a Bronze Star.

Upon his return, he was not unplugged. In Oklahoma he killed 168, among them women and children. "They're collateral damage," he said.

But they didn't pin another medal on his chest. They gave him a lethal injection. And he was discharged.

# Earth in Flames

In the predawn hours of February 13, 1991, two smart bombs blew apart an underground military base in a neighborhood of Baghdad.

But the base wasn't a base. It was a bomb shelter filled with sleeping people. In a few seconds, it became a funeral pyre. Four hundred and eight civilians were burned to a crisp. Among them were fifty-two children and twelve infants.

Khaled Mohammed's entire body was an open wound. He thought he was dead, but he wasn't. Crawling on hands and knees, he managed to get out. He couldn't see. The fire had sealed his eyelids shut.

The world couldn't see either, because TV was too busy exhibiting the new killing machines being launched on the market.

# Thundering Sky

After Iraq came Yugoslavia.

From afar, from Mexico, Aleksander listened on the phone to the fury of war over Belgrade. When the telephones worked, and they did off and on, he heard the voice of Slava Lalicki, his mother, barely audible over the roar of bombs and the wail of sirens.

Missiles were raining on Belgrade, and every blast echoed again and again in Slava's head.

Night after night, for seventy-eight nights in the spring of 1999, she could not sleep.

When the war ended, she still couldn't. "It's the silence," she said. "This insufferable silence."

# The Other Warriors

While missiles were endured by Yugoslavia, celebrated on television, and sold in toy stores everywhere, two boys achieved the dream of a war of their own.

Since they had no enemy, they made do with whoever was at hand. Eric Harris and Dylan Klebold killed thirteen and left their high school cafeteria littered with the wounded. This happened in Littleton, Colorado, a town that relies on a missile factory owned by Lockheed Corporation. Eric and Dylan did not use missiles. They used pistols, rifles, and bullets they'd purchased at a local department store. After killing, they killed themselves.

The media reported that they'd also planted two propane bombs to blow up the school and everyone in it, but the bombs did not go off.

The other crazy plan they hatched was barely noted. These two death-loving boys wanted to hijack a plane and crash it into the twin towers in New York.

# Welcome to the New Millennium

Two and a half years after that high school bullet-fest, New York's twin towers collapsed like dry sand castles.

The terrorist attack killed three thousand workers.

President George W. Bush was thus given a license to kill. He declared eternal war, a world war against terrorism, and soon invaded Afghanistan.

This terrorist attack killed three thousand peasants.

Bursts of flame, explosions, howls, curses; TV screens were seething. Every day they replayed the tragedy of the twin towers, intertwined with the blast of bombs falling on Afghanistan.

In a town somewhere, far from this global madness, Naúl Ojeda was sitting on the floor with his three-year-old grandson. The boy said, "The world doesn't know where its house is."

They were looking at maps.

They could have been looking at the news.

# Newscast

The entertainment industry thrives on the loneliness market.
The consoling industry thrives on the anguish market.
The security industry thrives on the fear market.
The lying industry thrives on the stupidity market.
How do they gauge their success? On the stock market.
The arms industry too. Their stock prices are the best news in every war.

# Global News

A few months after 9/11, Israel bombed Jenin.

The Palestinian refugee camp was reduced to an immense hole in the ground, filled with bodies and wreckage.

Jenin's hole was the same size as the one left by the twin towers.

Apart from the survivors sifting through the debris in search of their loved ones, how many people saw it?

# Eternal War

As was his habit, the president of the planet thought things through:

To do away with forest fires, cut down the forests.

To cure a headache, cut off the head.

To liberate the Iraqis, bomb them to smithereens.

So, after Afghanistan, it was Iraq's turn.

Iraq yet again.

The word *oil* did not come up.

# Objective Information

Iraq was a threat to humanity. Saddam Hussein was responsible for 9/11. Any day now that terrorist tyrant might drop an atom bomb on your street.

That's what they said. Later on, the truth came out. The only weapons of mass destruction were the speeches that made them up.

Those speeches lied, and so did the television, the papers, and the radio.

Smart bombs, however, dumb as they seem, did not lie. By disemboweling unarmed civilians in the fields and on the streets of the invaded country, smart bombs told the truth about war.

## Orders

It happened on September 11 in the year 2001, when the airplane hijacked by terrorists slammed into the second of New York's twin towers.

The instant the tower began to tremble, people dashed for the stairs.

Suddenly, midexodus, the loudspeakers came on.

The loudspeakers ordered everyone back to work.

Those who did not obey improved their chances of survival.

# The Gunner

The prime minister of Israel made the decision. His defense minister conveyed it. The head of the army explained that they were going to use chemotherapy against the Palestinian cancer. The brigade general declared a curfew. The colonel ordered the hamlets and the planted fields to be razed. The division commander sent in tanks and blocked access to ambulances. The captain gave the order to start shooting. The lieutenant told the gunner to fire the first missile.

But the gunner, that particular gunner, was not there. Yigal Bronner, the final link in the chain of command, had been sent to prison for refusing to go on killing.

# Another Gunner

A bricklayer since childhood. When he turned eighteen, he had to stop working to do his military service.

They assigned him to the artillery brigade. One day during target practice, he was ordered to shoot at an empty house.

A house like any other, sitting by itself in the countryside. He had learned how to aim, but he could not bring himself to do it. They screamed out the order a second time, but he just couldn't.

He had built quite a few houses like that one. He could have explained that a house has legs rooted in the ground, and a face like in a child's drawing, eyes for windows, a mouth for a door, and deep inside a soul left by those who built it and memories of everyone who lived in it.

He could have explained all that, but he didn't say a thing. If he had, they would have shot him for idiocy. He stood at attention and remained silent. He ended up in the clink.

Carlo Barbaresi tells this story to a group of friends around a campfire in the mountains of Argentina. It's about his father in Italy, back in the time of Mussolini.

# And Yet Another

It wasn't just any Sunday afternoon in 1967.

It was the afternoon of the classic. Club Santafé against Millonarios, and the entire city of Bogotá was in the stands. Outside the stadium there was nobody except the crippled and the blind.

The match seemed to be headed for a tie. Then Omar Lorenzo Devanni, the Santafé striker, fell. The referee whistled a penalty kick.

Devanni was bewildered. No one had touched him; he simply tripped. He wanted to tell the referee it was a mistake, but the Santafé players picked him up and carried him on a stretcher to the white penalty spot. There was no way out of it. The stadium was roaring, on the edge of delirium.

Between the posts, the hangman's posts, waited the keeper.

Devanni placed the ball on the white spot.

He knew what he was going to do and the price he was going to pay. He chose ruin; he chose glory: Devanni took a running start and with all his might kicked it wide, far wide of the goal.

# Time Weighs

Four and a half centuries ago in Geneva, they used green wood to burn Miguel Servet alive. He had gone there to escape the Inquisition, but Calvin sent him to the stake.

Servet believed no one should be baptized before becoming an adult, he had doubts about the mystery of the Holy Trinity, and he stubbornly insisted on teaching that blood flows through the heart and is purified in the lungs.

His heresies condemned him to the life of a gypsy. Before they caught up to him, he'd changed countries, homes, trades, and names many times.

Servet was burned on a slow fire along with the books he had written. On the cover of one of them was an engraving of Sampson carrying a tremendously heavy door on his back. Underneath, it said, "I carry my freedom with me."

# Time Passes

Six centuries after its founding, Rome decided that the year would begin on the first day of January.

Before then, years began on March 15.

The date had to be changed for reasons of war.

Spain was on fire. The rebellion, which challenged the empire's might and devoured thousands upon thousands of legionaries, obliged Rome to change the tally of its days and the cycles of its affairs of state.

The uprising lasted many long years until at last the city of Numantia, capital of the Hispanic rebels, was besieged, vanquished, and burned to the ground.

Its remains lie on a hill, surrounded by fields of wheat at the edge of the Duero River. Of the city that changed the world's calendar forever, practically nothing is left.

But when we raise our glasses at midnight every December 31, we drink a toast to her, whether or not we realize it: may there always be another year and people who are free.

# Time

We are daughters and sons of the days. "What is a person in the road?"

"Time."

The Maya, ancient masters of such mysteries, have not forgotten that we come from time and are made of time, which is born with every death.

And they know that time reigns supreme and it laughs whenever money tries to buy it,

surgery tries to erase it,

pills try to silence it,

and machines try to measure it.

But when the rebellious Indians of Chiapas sat down to talk peace, a Mexican government official had their number. Pointing to his own wrist and to those of the Indians, he decreed: "We use Japanese watches, and you use Japanese watches. For us it is nine in the morning, and for you it is nine in the morning. So stop pestering me with all this nonsense about time."

# Hard Times

When the season is the enemy, bearing black skies and days of ice and storms, the newborn alfalfa sits quietly and waits. The timid sprouts go to sleep, and in their slumber they survive while the hard times last, no matter how long that may be.

When sunny days finally come and the skies turn blue and the ground begins to warm, the alfalfa awakens. Then, only then, does it grow. It grows so fast you can see it, pushed up from the roots by gusts not made of air.

# The Light Soars

In the mountains of Cajamarca, amid the peaks that took the longest to awaken and arise when the world was born, there are many figures painted by artists without names.

Those colorful tattoos on rock faces have survived for thousands of years, despite the ravages of weather.

The paintings are or aren't, according to the time of day. Some catch fire when the day begins and go out by noon. Others change shape and color throughout the long march of the sun from dawn to dark. Still others appear only with dusk.

The paintings were created by human hand, but they are also works of light, the light that time sends day after day, and they are at her beck and call. She, the light, that other artist, queen and lady, conceals them and unveils them as and when she wishes.

# The Challenge

The largest birds in the world fly not in the sky but in the ground.

They were sketched by the ancient inhabitants of Nazca, who knew how to summon marvels from the bare desert.

Seen from the ground, the lines say nothing. They are but long canals of stone and dust, which vanish in the distance on that high plain of dust and stone.

Seen from the air, those wrinkles in the desert form gigantic birds with outstretched wings.

The drawings are two or two and a half thousand years old. Airplanes, as far as we know, did not exist. For whom were they made? For whose eyes? Experts disagree.

I think, I wonder, could those perfect lines, which glisten in the dry air, have been born so the heavens could see them?

The heavens offer us their splendid designs, etched with stars or clouds, and it's only right that we show our appreciation. The earth is not incapable. Perhaps that is what those people who turned the desert into a masterpiece wished to say: that the earth, too, can draw the way the heavens draw, and can fly without ever leaving the ground, on the wings of the birds it creates.

# Day Is Born

He's always first. When the end of night approaches, silence is broken by the one out of tune. The one out of tune, the bird who never tires, awakens the master singers. And before first light, all the birds in the world begin their serenade at the window, sailing over the flowers, over their reflections.

A few sing for love of the art. Others broadcast news or recount gossip or tell jokes or give speeches or proclaim delight. But all of them, artists, reporters, gossips, wags, cranks, and crazies, join in a single orchestral overture.

Do birds announce the morning? Or, by singing, do they create it?

# ABOUT THE AUTHOR

EDUARDO GALEANO is one of Latin America's most admired writers, as well as a distinguished journalist and historian. The winner of the first Lannan Foundation Cultural Freedom Prize in 1998, he is the author of *Upside Down,* the *Memory of Fire* trilogy (for which he won the 1989 American Book Award), *Open Veins of Latin America,* and many other works. He lives in Montevideo, Uruguay.